ONLY YOUR
HEART
CAN HEAL
YOU

ONLY YOUR HEART CAN HEAL YOU

How Ayahuasca Helped Me Survive Cancer

JASNA CLANCY

Redwood Publishing, LLC

Paperback ISBN: 978-1-947341-73-9
eBook ISBN: 978-1-947341-74-6
Library of Congress Catalogue Number: 2019910290

Published & Designed by Redwood Publishing, LLC
(Orange County, California)

Interior Design: Ghislain Viau
Cover Design: Michelle Manley

First Printing. Printed in the United States of America

10 9 8 7 6 5 4 3 2 1

Shawn, My Incredible Husband,
Without Your Love, I Would Not Have Survived.

Disclaimer

This book discusses the medical use of Ayahuasca, a potentially mind-altering substance. The author wants to make it clear that no one should use Ayahuasca—or any other such substance—for medical purposes or for any other purpose without the immediate, direct supervision of a competent licensed physician who is an expert in these matters. The dangers of using any such substances without skilled medical supervision are serious. Nothing in this book is meant to suggest the appropriateness of using such substances for any purpose at any time without the direct, specific care of a proper, licensed, and knowledgeable physician.

Contents

CHAPTER 1

Just Another Sunny Day

It was a beautiful summer day in Marina del Rey, California, and I was having a wonderful time at the pool with my little niece and nephew. I was living not just the good life, but a glorious life. At fifty-one years old, I had married the man of my dreams the year before. My work was very gratifying and meaningful. I felt healthy, strong, and at peace. Frankly, I had no idea such happiness was possible.

I decided to take the children for lunch, right across the street to the Cheesecake Factory. Before long we were seated in a comfy booth. Seven-year-old Marko and his little sister, four-year-old Bianca, were indulging in their pasta while I was cheerfully munching away on my favorite menu item, the avocado egg rolls.

Not having children of my own, I took special joy in my close relationship with my brother, Vladimir, his wife, Alice, and their adorable children. We were talking about the fun activities we could do together during the summer when I heard my phone ring from inside my handbag. It was a doctor calling from the pathology lab at Kaiser.

"Mrs. Clancy, we have the report back from your biopsy, and I need to tell you that you have breast cancer." Her words echoed in my head. "It is a pre-invasive, high-grade DCIS tumor. It is contained; however, it is very large and concerning. It is 8.6 centimeters, or about 3.4 inches. You need to call your doctor right away about the next steps."

I was in such a state of shock that I had to keep asking her to repeat what she was saying. Was it the background noise of the lunch crowd at the restaurant that was blocking me from hearing her, or was it the terrifying word *cancer* that suddenly took up all the space in my head?

* * *

A few weeks earlier I had felt something hard and flat on my right breast, something about the size of a quarter, so of course, I had it checked out. I wasn't too worried; I had undergone breast-enhancement surgery years earlier. It had been botched and needed to be redone, so I figured the hard spot in my breast was only calcification.

Other than having just learned I had cancer, I was the picture of health and took great care of myself. Between working out three to four times a week at the gym, walking on the beach, rollerblading, and biking, I was rather fit. My husband, Shawn, and I ate mostly organic, vegetarian food, and we meditated regularly. I never smoked and never used any drugs. Simply, I did everything right.

A year before I met Shawn, I ended an emotionally abusive and destructive ten-year roller-coaster relationship that had left me drained. Miraculously, I was now married to the love of my life, and I'd never felt this depth of love before. Honestly, I had it all!

We lived in a twelfth-floor condo with a spectacular view of the Pacific Ocean. (Growing up in gloomy German winters, I appreciated every sunny California day.) Shawn was able to work from home, so we got to spend much of our time together. I was happier than I had ever been before.

It's not that I thought I was immune to cancer: I didn't think, *Why me?* But I did think, *Why now?*

I hung up the phone, still stunned and shaking, and began to cry.

Marko asked, "Why are you crying, Teta?" (My brother and I are originally from Croatia, and his children speak Croatian with me. *Teta* means "aunt.") I don't even remember what I said to him, but I immediately called Vladimir and told him to come pick up the children as soon as possible. Almost robotically, I told them, "Come on, we have to go," and they followed me dutifully toward the door, even though they had not finished eating. I heard our waiter calling loudly to me, "Ma'am, you haven't paid your bill!"

I turned to him with tears in my eyes and said in a daze, "I'm sorry. I just got a call from my doctor's office that I have cancer," and then fumbled in my wallet for cash to pay the check. The waiter was so caring that he actually hugged me and told me how sorry he was.

My brother came within minutes to collect his kids. He embraced me compassionately, telling me he knew I would be all right. Trembling and shaking, I walked across the street and took the elevator up to our condo. I pulled Shawn from his office into our bedroom so that his teenage daughter, Maddy, wouldn't hear the crushing news right away. Between sobs I told him about the call.

He held me firmly and said, "Don't worry, Angel." (He always calls me Angel.) "We will get through this together. You are going to be okay."

But I was devastated and scared, crying both out of panic and out of gratitude for Shawn's love for me and for his support. Would I really lose this wonderful life so soon, now that it was finally mine?

When you are diagnosed with cancer, your whole world collapses, and all your dreams are immediately shattered. In one split second, I was faced with death and filled with an all-encompassing terror.

This story is about my profound journey through two bouts of cancer over two years and the deep insights I gained about fear, resentment, anger, forgiveness, and love. I was relentless in pursuing non-traditional healing modalities in addition to traditional Western methods. The non-traditional approaches taught me a great deal about my emotional life.

My cancer journey took me on an unexpected trip and changed my life forever. And, while I would never wish cancer or any other illness on anyone, I have to say that cancer was a blessing in disguise and the best thing that ever happened to me and to my family.

In the following pages, I want to take you with me on a journey and reveal the tools that helped me heal. I hope this book will inspire you towards your own healing and towards greater health, overall happiness, and deeper love.

CHAPTER 2

From Fear to Empowerment

After receiving the shocking, life-altering phone call, both Shawn and I were unable to sleep that night. We were confronted with paralyzing fear due to the emotional and physical challenges we were about to face. Coincidentally, Shawn's first wife had endured breast cancer twice, and now as my husband, he had to go through this for the third time. He felt devastated, afraid, and angry all at the same time.

The next day I made an appointment with the oncology department at Kaiser. When Shawn and I arrived for our meeting with Dr. Takasugi, a general surgeon, she had some good news.

"You have a bit of time to decide how you want to proceed," she told us. "The cancer is not aggressive, but regardless, we do need to take it out. You'll need surgery as well as chemotherapy, and perhaps radiation."

"I don't want to do any of that," I announced to the doctor. "I'm going to try to take care of it myself."

To her credit, Dr. Takasugi did not appear impatient or annoyed. Instead, she looked at me thoughtfully for a moment before responding.

"I respect that you want to look at alternative healing options." She paused. "But, if you don't have the surgery and the chemo, I'm afraid the tumor might become aggressive. The size is very concerning. Take some time, but don't take too long."

Shawn fully supported my decision to pursue holistic healing methods. We were committed to living a healthy lifestyle, and both of us had been extremely fortunate to be in excellent health. We seldom were sick, and I rarely even had a headache.

When I was about ten years old, my parents shifted to a more health-conscious lifestyle. This change happened because my father, at the age of thirty-four, had developed some ulcer problems. He was told to drastically cut down on red meat, so my mother put us all on a vegetarian diet emphasizing whole grains and vegetables. My parents treated us with alternative medicine and only took us to Western-trained physicians when they felt it was absolutely necessary. Eventually my father became a holistic medical practitioner in Germany.

With this background, it was simply second nature for me to look first at alternative approaches to treat my cancer.

At least I wasn't as radical as my mother, who was diagnosed with breast cancer in 2004. While the tumor was very small, she ignored the doctor's advice to have surgery, choosing instead to "starve" her cancer by literally starving *herself.* For forty-three days—yes, forty-three days—she survived on water alone and absolutely nothing else. Her tumor eventually disappeared, but a year later, another lump showed up. This time we insisted she have the surgery, and she did; however, she refused chemotherapy, even though they found cancer cells in her lymph nodes. Fortunately, even without chemo or any other treatments, she has remained cancer-free ever since.

I understand and appreciate the astonishing achievements of conventional medicine. Western-trained doctors save lives every day, and I thank God for their knowledge. Nonetheless, my first choice, whenever possible, is to go the holistic healing route.

My parents had taught me that all things happen for a reason, and that there is something spiritual to learn from every experience. They had been atheists in their twenties and thirties—not surprising, since they had been born and raised under Communist rule in the former Yugoslavia. As my parents discovered holistic medicine and more natural ways of eating, my father began exploring Eastern philosophy. They eventually adopted certain Hindu practices and even sang us songs in Sanskrit! My father became a teacher of Transcendental Meditation® and often advised us, "Go within. Be quiet. Listen to what your soul is telling you."

* * *

I came to the United States with my first husband in 1989. We were both in our twenties and eager to make it in America, but our marriage ended after only a few years. I spent my mid-thirties and well into my forties in unsatisfying relationships, including a ten-year, on-again, off-again relationship with a man I shall call "Derick." We started a business together and were even engaged for a time. But it was an unstable and emotionally destructive relationship that involved yelling, cursing, and constant criticism and blame. There were other women involved endlessly, and instead of building me up, he persistently undermined my confidence. After a decade of feeling undesirable, inadequate, and never physically acceptable, I finally had the courage to move on.

Despite this unlucky track record in romance, I was ready to try again when I returned to Los Angeles in January 2013. I had spent the previous four years in my native Croatia, where I had a healing practice for a treatment called AtlasProfilax®. My brother, Vladimir, and I became practitioners in Switzerland and were working throughout Europe. AtlasProfilax delivers amazing results with headaches, neck pain, and back pain. I absolutely love my work! My job is all about healing people and making a difference in their lives.

Back in California, after having been single and extremely lonely in Croatia, I was ready for a new relationship. I joined a few online dating websites. In my profile I had written that

I wanted someone comfortable in his masculinity, who would help me tap into my feminine energy, which had apparently been on vacation for quite some time. My headline read: "You wear the pants; I wear the panties."

After many mismatches, Shawn contacted me through OKCupid.com. He had not bothered to upload a flattering photo or even to say much about himself in his profile, so I ignored him. In a second message, he wrote, "I get the 'feminine essence' comment in your profile, and I'm intrigued that you are aware of what that can do for a relationship. As a man, I know it's important to have contrasting energy . . . so I will bring the masculine part."

I ignored him again. In his third attempt to get me to reply, he wrote something clever and captivating: "I am reminded how beautiful the silence can be with the right person." This put a smile on my face, and I agreed to meet him for a drink.

That day, however, I found myself regretting my decision. I wasn't in the mood to meet a new man, nor was I in the mood to get dressed up or put on any makeup. Nevertheless, I had promised to meet him, so I went, arriving at the Mercedes Bar & Grille in Marina del Rey a few minutes late.

It was 7:15 p.m. on March 19, 2013, when Shawn came over and introduced himself. I was stunned. Shawn's sincerity was immediately apparent, and he looked much better than his online photo. (Who puts an unflattering picture of himself on a dating website?!) He gave me a brilliant and genuine smile. My attitude totally changed as I began to feel the strong chemistry and attraction between us.

We had many things in common. We were both vegetarian, and both liked David Deida's books about masculine and feminine polarities. The date that I had been determined to end within sixty minutes ended up lasting three and a half hours. Shawn had recently ended a two-year relationship, and I admired the way he described the "conscious breakup" that he and his former girlfriend had participated in with a trained facilitator. He took full responsibility for what had gone wrong. In doing so, he experienced completing that relationship with integrity, which left him free and available to attract the woman of his dreams—me!

Shawn was fully present and focused that evening. He never looked at his phone or interrupted me when I answered his questions about my life. Only later did he tell me that he had even been synchronizing his breathing to match mine. That's how connected he felt from the start. He wasn't trying to impress me, and we were laughing a lot throughout the evening.

"So, who f***ed up and made you single?" he asked with a grin.

I gave him a shortened rundown of my romantic history. At the end of the date, he thoughtfully took my hand before we crossed the street, ensuring my safety and making me feel taken care of.

After that first date, whenever he'd call and I'd see his number on my phone, I would get butterflies in my stomach, and a smile would automatically appear on my face. That's when I knew he was the one.

Eleven months later, we stood side by side at a beautiful chapel in Las Vegas surrounded by family and friends as we said our vows on the brink of joyful tears. Six years later (and counting), we continue to fall in love, deepening our affection with every passing day and complementing each other with the masculine and feminine polarities. He enjoys telling me, "I'm still falling, baby."

* * *

Shawn was my full partner in everything—including my cancer journey. We began watching a video series called *The Truth About Cancer*, which features interviews with medical doctors and practitioners of alternative medicine. These included homeopathy and naturopathy, as well as interviews with patients who had been cured of cancer through a variety of natural and holistic methods. We were fascinated and inspired.

I was also exploring the best way to understand what was going on in my inner emotional life. One doctor who was interviewed in the series said that the first thing you should do after a cancer diagnosis is to make a list of people you need to forgive—and to forgive them. He stated, "Holding grudges and resentments are extremely toxic to the body." I began to think about that carefully.

Based on what we learned from that program, I stopped eating all sugar and refined carbohydrates. I began juicing every day with organic fruits and vegetables, and making meals out of raw foods. I was even growing my own sprouts. Oh my goodness, it was so time-consuming! It would practically take up my entire day.

During the first six months, I did regular cleanses, including colonics and coffee enemas, and I was taking powerful supplements from a company called Frequency Foods that included large amounts of probiotics, vitamin C, vitamin E, minerals, and enzymes. I also incorporated high-alkaline, 11.5 pH Kangen water. Additionally, I meditated, wrote a gratitude list, and lay on a PEMF (Pulsed Electromagnetic Field) therapy mat to increase the blood flow throughout my body for twenty minutes every morning.

Soon I began calling cancer my "health opportunity," a phrase I'd learned at the Optimum Health Institute in San Diego. Along with my cancer-fighting diet, cleanses, and detoxifications, I was also trying to find out why cancer had manifested in my body. What did I need to learn from it? How could I find the answers to the questions that plagued me, "*Why me, and why now?*" As my parents had taught me, I understood that even cancer had something to teach me, and I sensed that there was a message deep within my soul that I needed to access.

Besides, the connection between emotional health and physical health is now pretty much universally acknowledged, so I felt more culturally supported in my determination to understand what kind of emotional issues might be affecting me "under the radar." I had to know what I had failed to deal with that could have been connected to the cancer taking root in my body. One book that impressed me on this topic was *When the Body Says No: Exploring the Stress-Disease Connection* by Dr. Gabor Maté. He draws on cutting-edge science, explaining that emotions are inseparable from our health, and repressed emotions bring on stress that could lead to disease.

It was extremely important to me to get as much information as possible in order to gain more control over this horrendous situation. But even with all the loving support and encouragement around me, I still would wake up in the middle of the night, thinking, *I have cancer!*

One day, I was sitting in a restaurant looking around at all the people eating their food and having a good time. I thought, *They don't know how lucky they are. None of them have cancer!* Of course, I couldn't know that for sure, yet that's how all-consuming these thoughts were; at times I could not see beyond my own anxieties. I sat among the other diners as if everything were normal, while inside I couldn't shake the fear of death that hung over me.

The first month was the worst, and Shawn and I had many sleepless nights. At first, right after my diagnosis, I put on a false happy face, telling people, "I'm going to be fine!" It was in my nature to protect other people's feelings, not wanting them to worry about me. Even though I couldn't shake the persistent presence of fear inside, I was very good at pretending I had it all under control. There were times when I would wake up in the middle of the night in a panic—my heart pounding fiercely—afraid I was having a heart attack. One night when I got up to go to the bathroom, I passed out and hit my head very hard on the tile floor.

Needless to say, the emotional stress from my cancer diagnosis was overwhelming. The fear that came along with it was unlike any other fear that I had ever experienced. Cancer had changed our lives overnight. It stole all my focus and energy, and there were moments when I felt like I was on death row.

Over time, listening and re-listening to alternative doctors gave me a lot of hope, and this helped my fears begin to recede. Knowing that many people heal from cancer, I chose to believe in the diagnosis, but not in the fatalistic prognosis. To help myself cope emotionally, I was determined to focus on a cure. I decided to hold tight to the optimistic thought, *I will be one of the cancer survivors!*

* * *

Since my life and work were put on hold, I called Lluis, a close friend in Bogotá, Colombia, who was a spiritually centered person and a facilitator of Ayahuasca ceremonies. Ayahuasca is a hallucinogenic brew made from vines indigenous to South America. For many centuries, it has been used by native people in ceremonies to promote healing and spiritual growth, and to transform one's experience of reality. At the time I began my dark dance with cancer, Ayahuasca and other forms of psychedelic therapy were already showing promise in treating illnesses ranging from depression and addiction to PTSD.

When Lluis heard I had cancer, he immediately said, "You need to come to Bogotá for a few Ayahuasca ceremonies. Come as soon as possible so you can address the emotional issues that will help you understand why you have attracted this cancer into your life. Deep within you is the answer, Jasna."

Five weeks after my diagnosis, Lluis picked us up from the El Dorado International Airport in Bogotá and drove us to his home. He was warm and welcoming. For three days before drinking Ayahuasca, we had to avoid all caffeine, alcohol, sugar, and fermented foods and eat lightly—just cooked vegetables and broths. He promised to feed us well after we'd completed all the ceremonies.

Many people rely on shamans (medicine men) to lead them in an Ayahuasca journey. Lluis was too humble and respectful of tradition to call himself a shaman, but because of his knowledge, skill, and experience, Shawn and I knew that we would be safe with him guiding our journey.

He showed us the guest room, which was prepared for the ceremony that would begin later that evening. There were two mattresses on the floor, where we would be lying for at least seven hours, with a small bucket next to each of them. It is common to purge when the "sacred plant medicine," as Ayahuasca is also called, begins to take effect. Lluis set up a small altar and showed us branches of dried sage, which would be used later to cleanse the environment.

The feeling was intimate and inviting, and I attempted to absorb the calming energy that Lluis had created for this space. But I couldn't quite do it; I was too nervous. I had never experienced any mind-altering states before, and my body is very sensitive to foreign substances. And though I was comforted that Lluis's wife was a medical doctor and would remain in the house, I was still having haunting thoughts: *What if my body has a bad reaction to this? What if something goes wrong? What if I go mad?* The fear that I might lose control of my mind while under the influence of a hallucinogenic plant just wouldn't go away. I was about to enter an intense phase of confronting my "health opportunity." Was I truly prepared mentally and emotionally? What would I see when the visions began?

In just a few short hours, I would find out.

CHAPTER 3

Me and "Mama Aya"

Lluis explained that the Ayahuasca brew is a combination of two different plants and contains DMT (N,N-Dimethyltryptamine). DMT is one of the most potent vision-inducing substances known and is used for profound spiritual transformations. The vine, Ayahuasca, is often referred to as the "the vine of the soul" and "the mother of all plants." It is said that the voice of higher intelligence that one hears during the ceremony is female and that "She" will give you exactly what you need. "She" is also called "Mama Aya." Lluis suggested that we participate in three consecutive Aya ceremonies, one each day.

That evening, Shawn and I sat in the calming, dimly lit room that felt secure and sacred. Feeling anxious of what was about to happen, I can't recall many specific details about the space. All I remembered was that a critical element of seeking guidance from this powerful plant was in the setting of specific intentions.

My intention was, of course, to get insights into why this *dis*-ease manifested in my body. "Please show me what I need to learn from this cancer," I requested of my consciousness. "Show me how to heal and serve my highest good."

Before we began, Lluis said a prayer in Portuguese while ritually waving a bundle of burning sage, with the purpose of purifying the energy. It was clear he had true reverence for this mysterious plant and was approaching the ceremony with great respect and humility.

We sat quietly on our mats, drawing in a few deep breaths in order to drop from our heads into our hearts and get present with our intentions. Still, I felt somewhat nervous. I knew that once I drank this magical drink, there would be no turning back. Lluis gave us each our first dose, just about an ounce. The potion was a thick molasses brew that tasted awful. The sulfurous, muddy-flavored sludge was almost unbearable to drink.

Somehow, I managed to get the gooey tea down. Remaining in a sitting position, we began to meditate. I felt prepared to make a connection with my Higher Self and to tap into my inner wisdom in order to receive the deepest level of healing.

About forty-five minutes had passed when Lluis came over and whispered, "Do you feel anything?"

I didn't. He gave me another dose. I barely got the liquid down, when—oh my God, my heart started pounding furiously, my head was buzzing intensely, and I was shivering tremendously as Ayahuasca was circulating inside me. I was overcome with terrifying thoughts: *Oh no! Why did I take that second dose? [Or, to be more precise, why the hell did I take Ayahuasca in the first place?!] That second dose hasn't even kicked in yet, and it's already bordering on the intolerable. How will I feel in another half hour, when it does kick in fully?* There was no going back! My stomach was upset to the point that I actually thought I might die.

Lluis was there to reassure me that everything that was happening was normal. I repeatedly vomited into the bucket. Even though only a few drops came out of my mouth, it felt as if I was expelling everything I had ever eaten in my entire life. My panic returned, and I thought, *This has all been a colossal mistake.*

Lluis came over and whispered, "Try to relax and focus on your breathing. Connect to your breath." It seemed as if hours and hours had passed since the second dose, when he informed me it had only been fifteen minutes.

I started to sense that "She" wanted me to meet "Her" halfway and to surrender fully.

Finally, after making peace with Mama Aya, my stomach settled. I lay down on my mat and covered myself with a blanket.

The feeling of sickness dissipated, and thankfully, I transitioned into a blissful, indescribable higher state of consciousness. Ayahuasca was expanding every aspect of my awareness, and I found myself in a mysterious altered and infinite realm with my heart wide open. There was no fear, no judgment, no expectation, no separation, only a peculiar sense of trust and Oneness. I felt connected to the Universe and *everything* in it; I *was* the Universe. My awareness of time and space was gone.

Unexpectedly, a huge, gorgeous flower petal with the brightest, most vibrant blue, pink, and purple colors stood like an enormous giant in front of me, swaying gently from side to side. It was majestically beautiful. "The vine of the soul" was revealing Herself in the most spectacular and exquisite way. I was mesmerized by the magnificence of it, when I heard a soft, sweet whisper, "There is nothing to be afraid of. We shall meet again tomorrow . . ." Shortly after that marvelous vision disappeared, I was left with deep peacefulness, and an incredible tranquility, excited for the next ceremony.

When it was all over, I hadn't gained any particular understanding, nor did I have any visions that satisfied my intentions. However, I was no longer afraid of the power of this magical plant.

* * *

When we had first decided to go to Bogotá, Shawn had been confronted with an overwhelming decision. He had been sober for over twenty-one years and regularly attended AA meetings. The thought of ingesting a mind-altering substance was unimaginable, and doing so would break his sobriety. It was a daunting and irrevocable decision.

I had made it clear that I had no expectations of him for this part of my journey.

After a few days of contemplating his options, he told me, "Angel, I am not willing to let you venture into the unknown by yourself. There is nothing I would not do for your healing, and that includes taking Ayahuasca."

Once he drank his first dose, and throughout the early part of the evening, Shawn became overly concerned with my well-being. Lluis insisted that he lay down on his mat, away from mine, to allow for his own experience.

"There is nothing to worry about, Shawn. I am here for Jasna. You need to have your own journey. Now, go within."

Unlike me, Shawn had remarkable visions and messages that night. The next day, as we were both processing and integrating, he shared with me his profound insights. Kevin, a lifelong friend, had suddenly appeared in his thoughts. Kevin had recently asked Shawn to write a testimonial letter on his behalf, as he was going through a divorce and needed a character reference for his child custody case.

"I fully intended to do it," Shawn shared with me, "but weeks went by, and I still hadn't written the letter. Here was a dear friend asking for my help, and I had procrastinated. I felt awful."

Right then in his journey, he became aware of the connection between this event and the other incidents in his life where he had said he was going to do something, but never did, as well as all the other things he had ever felt guilty for. All these moments of regrets, throughout his entire life, were right there in front of him.

"In came a vision of a large, old chest made of wood and iron," Shawn continued. "On the top of it the words clearly read, 'Not Going to Forgive Myself For.' There it was—the place I would store everything I could never forgive myself for—all of life's failures that validated my unworthiness. Then I heard an angelic, female voice gently whispered, 'Do you want to open it?' Startled by the question, I paused, afraid of what must lie inside. After some deliberation I finally said, 'Yes.'"

Shawn took a moment, as if reliving the experience.

"It was occurring in slow motion as I hesitantly reached out and grabbed the top edge. Gradually, I opened the chest and was astounded by what I saw—or didn't see. It was empty! *There was nothing inside.* And then, a wave of tenderness swept over me as I received the message, 'There is nothing to forgive.' I was overcome with a profound clarity. There was nothing to do, but bask in the purity of the moment. I was blessed, not just with divine insight, but also with a transforming revelation. There was nothing from my past for which I could not forgive myself. Self-love flooded my entire being and healing occurred in an instant. Ayahuasca revealed to me, in the kindest and gentlest way, where I stored my pain and the part of myself I had been denying all my life."

Of course, as soon as we returned home, Shawn wrote an amazing recommendation letter for his friend. He later said, "To compare Aya with recreational drugs is absurd. What it truly is, is an extremely powerful medicine and teacher."

* * *

The next day, Lluis drove us three hours outside of Bogotá to a charming home high on a hill in a tranquil remote area overlooking a scenic valley filled with palm trees. The house was a light terra-cotta color, with a lovely pool and a kitchen on a covered a patio that was completely open to the back of the property. There was a long wooden table with chairs painted in various cheerful colors.

That evening, our second ceremony was set up outside on the large patio with a breathtaking view of the tropical forest. As the sun was setting, we could hear charming songs of native birds in the distance. This time, Lluis had invited two of his assistants, Carlos and Arturo, to participate. Just like the evening before, he prepared the sacred space perfectly. I was not afraid any longer, just eager and thrilled to start.

We sat in a circle, ready to begin. Lluis whispered a prayer and made some beautiful whistling sounds as he blew tobacco smoke from a cigar onto the Aya potion. Pure, organic tobacco leaves play a big role in these ceremonies. They are used to protect the sacred space from what may be perceived as potentially bad spirits.

When it was time, Lluis invited me to take a seat in front of him.

After he blew several puffs of tobacco smoke into the small shot glass, half-filled with the mysterious tea, he offered it to me and said, "May you have a profound journey."

My hands moved into a prayer position with great respect and gratitude, while I bowed in honor of the plant medicine. With my eyes closed, I held the small glass in my hands for a few seconds to recall my intentions before chugging it down in one big sip.

We lay down on our individual mats and waited. Lluis had turned off the lights and softly began to sing calming, heart-opening South American songs called *Icaros*. The purpose of these songs was to guide and connect us to the spirit of the plant. This music was specially written to enhance the power of these ceremonies and is the driving force for deeper revelations. As I felt the light summer breeze and the vibrational waves of the *Icaros*, I started to drop into a deeply, relaxed state of being. An intense tingling sensation circled throughout my entire body as I was welcoming Mama Aya in.

While I continued to anticipate my insights and relax into Her, it was already time for the second round. As with the previous night, the second dose affected me quickly and powerfully. I had eaten very little during the day and was clean from all my vomiting the evening before. Regardless, I was consumed with the urge to purge. Nothing was coming out of me, though once again, I felt like I was vomiting up the world. And, just as before, I was in pain, with my head buzzing, followed by a crashing wave of heat sweeping over me, and my heart pounding forcefully. While I attempted to surrender, an intense, energetic, excruciating, epic purge blasted out of me. Letting go and releasing control were my biggest challenges. Inhaling and exhaling slowly and deeply, I was trying to yield and let Mother Ayahuasca come to me.

Then, similarly to the previous evening, as I was letting down my guard, it quickly shifted into an enormously deep inner peace. I was in a different dimension, accessing my Higher Self, while being completely aware of my surroundings.

Across the circle, Arturo was purging violently. I was present to his process, but I wasn't affected by it. It felt as if Mama Aya was wrapping Her arms around me, while the Universe was opening the gates of heaven and filling me with more love than I ever knew existed. I cannot adequately put it into words; I was both seeing the divine and becoming immersed in the divine.

Then, slowly, an image began to appear to my right. I recognized a former boyfriend, whom I will call "Peter," because he was the classic Peter Pan, a man who refused to grow up. While I was in a relationship with Peter, I had to arrange everything for him. I set him up with his own business—with *my* money, which he did not seem obliged to pay back. His mother had always taken care of him, and he expected the same from me. After many months of paying for everything and feeling taken advantage off, I broke up with him. I had not consciously thought about Peter in a long time and was very surprised that he'd showed up in my most blissful state.

"The vine of the soul" was pulling from my subconscious mind and revealing some past, long-forgotten memories for me to examine and explore. Instantly, I understood how much resentment I was still carrying toward Peter for the way he had used me—and for the way I had *let* him use me. All that anger was closing my heart and not serving me.

Almost as soon as I became aware of this resentment, I was swiftly overwhelmed with limitless love toward Peter. All I wanted was to offer him blessings and wish him only the best. I saw that little of it was his fault. His mother had never given him the skills to become a mature adult, and he was maintaining a lifestyle he had no desire to alter. I heard a gentle, kind voice telling me that, aside from his immaturity, he was a good person who didn't deserve my ongoing, although subconscious, ill will. Slowly, that image changed as I saw him sleeping in his bed, dreaming about me. Kneeling at his bedside and holding his hand, I was able to freely release him into immeasurable love.

The vision of Peter began to fade away to my right, while to my left, my former fiancé Derick appeared. The decade I had spent with him had caused me immense heartache, and I looked back on it as wasted time—ten whole years invested in a man who had behaved selfishly and, at times, even cruelly. Although I had been young and objectively quite attractive, Derick always made me feel inadequate. Thinking back, it's astonishing how I so readily accepted this behavior. He made remarks about my figure, especially my weight (I was a size four). What I thought was a rather cute butt was not firm enough; my weight was 125, rather than 118; my hands were not small enough and supposedly looked too masculine.

All those remarks confirmed for me that, indeed, I could never be attractive enough, sexy enough, or desirable enough. In trying to be the woman of Derick's dreams, I even had breast enhancement surgery. My Highest Self was reminding me how obsessed I had been with my looks all my life, and not surprisingly, I'd only attracted men who would reflect those insecurities back to me. There was another boyfriend who was so afraid I would gain weight, that every time we ate at a restaurant, he would make a point of saying, "You're not going to eat all that bread, are you?"

Derick was living by the compulsion that "The grass is greener on the other side." He was endlessly infatuated with other women and broke my heart countless times by sleeping with them. Still, I took him back over and over again, until even I could see what a doormat I had become. The very day we broke up, he began dating the receptionist in the business we ran together, and before long, she was pregnant. I faced them day after day at the office, yet I lived in denial of what it was doing to me. My mantra became, "I'm fine; I'm over it." I told this to myself and to close friends who asked me how I was able to deal with it all.

During that Aya journey, I saw this gigantic, dark cloud of resentment that had built up over *ten* years. It was so toxic! I realized that for all those years I had held enormous, deep-seated, and suppressed animosity toward Derick, preceded by more years of resenting Peter Pan. I felt terribly mistreated. I had agreed to do things I didn't want to do and blamed Derick for it, when, in fact, no one had put a gun to my head and made me do anything. I was entirely disconnected from honoring my own feelings. I could see how I had betrayed myself every time I would say "yes" when I wanted to say "no." No matter how difficult something was for me, I would "take it on," suppressing and denying my emotions just to make it through the day.

By constantly pretending to be strong and concealing the fact that things did not bother me, when, in fact, they did—significantly, I was depriving others of the opportunity to support me. I repeatedly insisted that everything was fine, even when I was hurting immensely. My entire way of being had been inauthentic—so inauthentic that I had convinced myself there were no negative feelings toward any of my former relationships. In truth, however, I had a massive reservoir of anger and resentment deeply rooted inside. These were the toxic, suppressed, and unaddressed emotions that had built up over many years. I was denying them on a daily basis, creating all those negative blockages that were bound to show up somewhere in my body.

And then I saw it—*Oh my God! My breast! Cancer had invaded my breast!* Of course, my breast, and not some other area. It was due to the way I treated myself, especially my breasts, which were never good enough for *me*. I had butchered my lovely breasts under the surgeon's knife to enhance them—three times. What oppressive criticism I had harbored towards myself and my precious, innocent body! My breasts represented the feminine part of myself, the part that I had neglected the most. *Undeniably, this was the area that demanded my greatest emotional healing.*

In that state of expanded consciousness, in the understanding of my True Self, everything was crystal clear. There was no blame, no resentment, no anger. My insecurities about not being "perfect" enough had nothing to do with Derick, nor with any other man.

By internalizing and objectively observing all those years of animosity and hurt, I unexpectedly discovered some magnificent gems of light hidden behind my resentments. Every heart-breaking incident carried a lesson for me to learn. In that deeply altered state, I had passed beyond the reaches of pain and regret. In one instantaneous moment, I was taught forgiveness, transforming resentment into compassion. That feeling of compassion had opened my heart. I was willing to bless those ten years with Derick, and I appreciated every single experience we had shared, even the hurtful ones. I took responsibility for all of them.

Unexpectedly, through *his* wounded heart, I saw only his humanity and goodness. I was willing to concede that he could be admirable and caring. All my bitterness for Derick evaporated. Surprisingly, so did all the jealousy I had harbored towards the other women who had become, unavoidably, part of our relationship. I felt myself embracing every one of them. I hugged Derick and thanked him for those harsh years of growth. His face appeared before me, and with my heart opened wide, I asked him to forgive me for holding him responsible for my lack of trust in men. I understood at last that, by staying too long in that relationship and by not giving voice to my own feelings, I had not honored or cherished myself. For the first time ever, I saw *my* responsibility as a contributor to all my relationships.

Strangely, I felt compassion for myself, too. I knew that I had done the best I could. And then—I forgave myself. In that moment, I realized that there was actually nothing to forgive. Because *when you turn resentment, blame, or self-judgment into compassion, there is nothing left.* True forgiveness is replacing judgment with empathy. When there is compassion, the heart opens, and there cannot be resentment or any negative emotions. *Suffering is nothing more than a closed heart.* I was overwhelmed with immeasurable love and acceptance.

That night, it became more than obvious as to why I had manifested this disease. One cannot separate the body from the mind. For me, all the unexpressed, buried resentment and rage, built up over many years, had made my system an inviting home for cancer cells. This "divine health opportunity" forced me to release all of it, to learn to forgive others, and above all to love and forgive myself.

These revelations gave me an unfathomable feeling of gratitude for my cancer. I kept on saying, "Thank you so much, Cancer, for showing up in my life so that I can transform this deep-seated resentment into compassion and heal myself. You came to teach me! What a blessing you are! Thank you! Thank you, Cancer." What I experienced for the first time in my life can only be described as pure bliss, pure love for everyone, for myself, and even for my cancer.

Hours later, sometime after two o'clock in the morning, I heard Lluis's voice announcing that it was time to close the ceremony. This second journey had been a profound and exceptional awakening. I opened my eyes feeling grounded, peaceful, and rejuvenated. Above all, I felt fearless.

* * *

The next day, Lluis suggested I do a tobacco cleanse. I wasn't sure what that meant or what more could possibly be left inside me to clean out. I won't go into details because, like the Ayahuasca brew, the tobacco cleanse involved drinking another thick, gooey, sludgy substance. The stuff was tobacco-based, and it made me just as sick as the Ayahuasca tea. I purged unknown substances for at least an hour. For the unexpected finale, Lluis actually blew some tobacco up my nostrils through a glass straw!

After that cleanse, sitting on the patio looking out at the picturesque, lush wilderness, I was so surprised at how much sharper and more detailed my vision was. Everything looked incredibly distinct, bright, and clear. I could see every line on every leaf far into the distance, and I felt an intense connection to it all. My entire being was focused and fully present.

To my astonishment, when I thought I could do no more, we did one more Ayahuasca event on the third day. Lluis asked me if I was ready to let the cancer go, and believe it or not, I said, "No!" Having gained such transformative insights, I thought if I released the disease, I would miss out on more needed processing and healing. I just wasn't ready to stop now. Cancer was serving me, and I decided to keep it until I had completed my emotional healing. I could now see that this process might take some time.

I set a new intention for the third ceremony: "Show me what else I need to do. Are there any more buried animosities and judgments that are holding me back? Is there anything from my childhood that needs healing?" I had a feeling something from that period would emerge if I allowed the mysterious medicine into my space one more time.

That evening I felt physically ill—even worse, if it can be imagined, than on the prior two nights. My stomach was empty, yet I was trying to purge with nothing coming out, while belching violently. My head was pounding so aggressively that I needed Lluis to help me to the bathroom so I could splash cold water on my face.

"Lluis, I can't take it anymore," I uttered in agony. "I'm so sick. I'm going to pass out." The world was spinning. Even with Lluis holding me and guiding me, I barely made it back to my mat. Somehow, once again I eventually surrendered to the pain. Gradually everything calmed down, allowing me to feel the deep connection to my Higher Self and the divine. I was starting to access the infinite place within me where healing was possible.

Lluis was playing some beautiful hymns in Portuguese, and by now I was familiar with the inner landscape to which I had surrendered. I saw my whole life before me and a new way of being.

That night, I did not get the answer to my question about what needed to be uncovered from my childhood. That would come later. Instead, I got more clarity about my self-image as a woman. My life had been one big obsession with my appearance. Like too many other women, I lived in a constant state of self-judgment and self-criticism. Why had I always been so hard on myself? Why was I always unhappy with the way I looked? Every time I saw my reflection in the mirror, I saw something I wanted to change or fix. Even at size four, I always imagined there were those last five pounds to lose. Those imaginary five pounds endlessly taunted me in order to satisfy my inner perfectionist. Never once had I really perceived myself as whole and complete, nor loved or appreciated myself! My body had never received a stamp of approval. I could not accept my "imperfections."

Consequently, of course, I was only attracting men who would reinforce what I was already telling myself: *You are not perfect enough, not beautiful enough, not good enough.*

The irony was that, to the outside world, I seemed remarkably confident, happy, and in control.

As I was deep in that expansive state of consciousness, I heard a tender whisper: "How would it feel if you were to love, value, and cherish your body and your true essence?"

Instantaneously, an immense gratitude for every cell exploded within me. "*YES. I love my body! I am so thankful for this fantastic, sturdy vessel! I love you, Jasna.*"

With this love and gratitude came acceptance of myself, acceptance of who I am. I was able to see myself as a beautiful, radiant being that didn't need to change anything. I understood that no matter how the body presented itself, it was always in a state of divine perfection, created to thrive when given love and appreciation. Mama Aya was revealing something I was slowly beginning to grasp. I could hear Her voice overtaking my entire being all the way into my cellular level:

Self-love is the most important love there is. Without self-love, you cannot forgive. Without self-love, you cannot love! Love yourself deeply.

Mother Ayahuasca was illuminating the unknown to me. She was presenting Herself as my teacher, my guide, and my mentor to unconditional self-love.

CHAPTER 4

Healing Heart

The Ayahuasca visions showed me what I needed to do so that I could heal emotionally, but I wondered if there was more under the surface that I had not touched upon during my ceremonies in Bogotá. It was my responsibility now to integrate the insights I'd gained into my daily life. I felt more liberated, grounded, and free. A sense of peacefulness filled me, and if any thoughts of my former boyfriends came to mind, only compassion was present. I could honestly say there was no bitterness or animosity left. I felt so light. What freedom!

All that deep-seated anger and resentment wouldn't have been released if I hadn't "walked in their shoes." The visions this powerful medicine revealed to me depicted the significant occurrences in their lives that had influenced their outlooks and behavior. As I watched the unfolding of their personal histories, I could see how Peter Pan's mother, "Wendy," had micromanaged and controlled everything he did throughout his entire life. As a child, his mother was emotionally absent, while providing for him financially and giving the appearance of being emotionally involved. As a result, he never felt loved.

Derick, on the other hand, was an African American boy who had been adopted into a white family in 1959. He'd never perceived himself as "different" until he started school, where he was rejected by both white and black children because he had a white family. The sense of rejection he lived with throughout his childhood and formative years created the man I came to know.

Observing the suffering that the men in my life had experienced allowed me to have empathy. I could then let go of my own pain. It is difficult—maybe impossible—to forgive someone who has hurt you badly without compassion for them. Mama Aya showed me that there are no "bad" people, just bad behavior, and that forgiveness was crucial for my emotional healing.

After Colombia, my sense of myself expanded as I started practicing more self-love. I could now experience a deeper connection with myself and, consequently, with others. I felt closer to my inner wisdom and recognized that an open heart was the best remedy I could give myself, and I sensed that *only my heart could heal me.*

I started nurturing my self-esteem on a daily basis. Every time I looked in the mirror, I would pause and acknowledge myself for my commitment to growth and self-love. I would smile, look into my eyes, and say, "I'm so proud of you for letting go of past anger, for learning to appreciate your body, for learning even to love your body for the first time ever."

I released all the negative messages I had absorbed from former partners. Now I was seeing myself in a new way, in a new light. Finally, I began to value my body for all it did for me each day and, yes, acknowledge its beauty. I also felt great joy for everything else I was so blessed to have: my husband, my family, and my life in America.

Shawn's love and devotion were above and beyond any I had ever experienced. It was clear to me now why cancer had appeared at the happiest time of my life. The depth of Shawn's love, and the powerful love between us, provided the strength I needed to go through it all. If such a disease would have shown up while I was in a relationship with any other man, I know without a doubt that I would not have survived. My heart overflows with deep gratitude just thinking about how loving, compassionate, and supportive Shawn and his daughters were throughout this challenging period. Shawn was with me every step of the way: every Ayahuasca ceremony, every doctor's appointment, and every meal I had, he was by my side. Having him as my husband during that time was the best thing that could have happened. It felt divinely orchestrated. Love is a beautiful Healer.

* * *

I was continuing my research on holistic healing. This led me to discover Dr. Thomas Lodi, an oncologist who had founded An Oasis of Healing, an integrative medical facility in Arizona. His program relies heavily on alternative cancer treatments, such as chelation therapy, colon hydrotherapy, ozone IVs, organic whole foods, and emotional healing.

We paid a visit to An Oasis of Healing and spoke to Dr. Lodi who asked me, "Why did you get cancer? If you don't know, it will be harder for us to help you."

I was happy to inform him that we'd gone to Colombia for three Ayahuasca ceremonies, and as a result, I understood why cancer manifested in my body.

"Great! Then you're already halfway there," he said. "The emotional aspect is crucial for healing. I believe you will be fine."

That's when I knew, *healing happens in your heart.*

We picked up several useful ideas from Dr. Lodi. One was the goal of turning my body into an entirely "cancer-intolerant" environment so it would stop growing cancer cells. This included absolutely no sugars or carbs (sugar is cancer's fuel), a completely raw foods diet, colonics, and regular injections of high-dose vitamin C and vitamin B-17, as well as ozone IVs (infused directly into my vein). Large doses of ozone are meant to fill the blood cells with oxygen to kill bacteria and boost the immune system. I found a physician back in L.A. who provided these types of injections and I had them regularly, according to Dr. Lodi's recommendation. I felt energized and really good after each ozone treatment.

My path toward healing physically and emotionally led me next to the Optimum Health Institute (OHI) in San Diego. Their philosophy of having the mind, body, and spirit work together in harmony was attractive to me. I signed up for their three-week program, and was quickly introduced to the phrase "health opportunity." They never used the word *cancer,* nor did they use the word *disease.* Whatever our reason for being there, they would refer to it by asking, "How is your health opportunity today?" It was a very positive and encouraging environment.

They emphasized making a gratitude list in the morning, which I did in conjunction with my daily affirmations. The act of writing down this list was important, empowering, and made it more real. I kept up my gratitude list for two years straight. Every morning before getting out of bed, I wrote down five things I was grateful for. It could be anything: our super comfortable bed, the amazing ocean view from our home, my wonderful husband, or the excellent raw food we had eaten the night before. As I stood in gratitude and visualized my healing, I would say, "Thank you for my strong, healthy, healing body."

Sometimes I acknowledged having a delicious green smoothie as I watched the sun set over the horizon of the Pacific Ocean. Or it could have been gratitude for waking up feeling especially uplifted. It might have been merely an inspiring conversation I had on the phone with my sister or my mother, perhaps a chance to visit with Vladimir and his family, or spending quality time with Paige and Maddy, Shawn's daughters. I felt so close to these beautiful young women that we began to refer to them as "our" daughters.

Of course, I wasn't always able to remain in that optimistic bubble. There were moments when doubt consumed me, days I didn't feel well, nights I didn't sleep. I sensed that despite all his encouragement, positive nature and ongoing support, Shawn remained enormously worried about me. He was faced with endless fear of the devastating possibility of losing me.

This undercurrent of panic afflicted both of us. There were moments when my courage failed me, and I was overcome with the intense terror of dying. I would think, *I have cancer. A lot of people die from cancer. I may only have a fifty-fifty chance of surviving this.* The thought tormented me that out of fifty-three challenging years on this planet, would I only be blessed with two fantastic years with Shawn? It seemed extremely unfair.

It was natural to experience days like that, but I had to make choices about my reaction to my situation moment by moment. When I was starting to feel afraid and depressed, I forced myself to shift my focus onto something good. Maybe I didn't feel so well that day, but I didn't have pain either. I coaxed my thoughts into a positive direction, knowing my thoughts created my reality. I may not have been able to jump over the canyon of despair instantly, but I could take small steps in reaching for a thought that felt a bit better than the previous one. I refused to be a victim.

Two of the most powerful words in the human language are "I am," so, in addition to keeping my gratitude list, I included "I am" statements. Whatever goes after those two words can powerfully shape our thinking. Reflecting upon what needed strengthening in my own mind, I would write such phrases as, "I am powerful. I am in perfect health. I am strong. I am committed. I am present. I am healing." Without fail, I wrote five or six different affirmations each day, one of the inspiring ideas I gained from reading two books by Louise Hay: *Love Yourself, Heal Your Life* and *Mirror Work*.

The OHI offered classes on emotional healing, creating a positive mental attitude, meditation, and raw "cooking." I learned new ways to prepare raw foods, including how to make my own wheatgrass juice, delicious nut crackers, seed dips, and "cookies"—raw energy bites—which I continue to make today. My whole family enjoys these treats.

Nevertheless, my sprouts-and-salad-only diet weakened me dramatically. By the end of my first week at the Institute, I lost ten pounds. I had no extra pounds to begin with, and felt physically exhausted, extremely depressed, and seriously weak.

Sobbing, I lamented to Shawn, "I just want a piece of toast! Why can't I just have one lousy piece of bread?"

Interestingly, by the end of the second week, I felt exceptionally energized, enthusiastic, and mentally alert—better than ever before. Remarkably, that feeling stayed with me for many months. Although admittedly, I never wanted to see another sprout for the rest of my life!

I particularly liked what they called the "releasing" ceremony on Fridays at OHI. About a hundred of us would gather around a small fire outside with our homework in hand. That homework was to write down everything we were ready to give up—things that were no longer serving us—and to throw that list into the flames, thereby releasing the past.

One day, getting ready for the releasing ceremony, I began to write, "I am ready to let go of my cancer," but my hand suddenly stopped. Similar to the experience I had in Bogotá, a little voice in my head protested.

"No. I'm not actually ready to release it. I'm getting a lot out of having this disease right now."

There was this wild, crazy thought that I still needed cancer to continue this amazing path of spiritual growth. It sounded absolutely insane that, as much as I feared cancer, part of me wanted to hold on to this deadly disease because it was notably transforming me on the deepest levels. I was learning to understand my feelings. I was growing spiritually, experiencing more love, and gaining a profound inner peace. I needed more time for this transformation. I did not want to stop this progress for any reason—yet.

Another significant improvement was in my capacity for patience. No one in my family would have disagreed with the statement that I had been an impatient person, the kind who was always eager for the next thing—the next goal, the next thrilling adventure, or the next sentence. If I was bored with someone's conversation, I let it show.

Now I was slowing down, taking time to evaluate myself, and discovering I wanted to be more present with the people in my life. I was ready to talk less and listen more.

Even though she lived in Canada and we only spoke on the phone, my sister, Zana, told me during one conversation, "Jasna, you've always been my best friend and were constantly there for me. But you know, you and I were always 'skimming' spirituality, never going beneath the surface. Since you were diagnosed with cancer, you really dove into the darkest corners of yourself and faced your biggest fears. It's really incredible to see your transformation. You are touching all our hearts—mine, Mom's, Dad's, Vladimir's, and Shawn's. You're bringing us all closer together. I'm excited to get to know the 'new you.'"

Ayahuasca was only one modality for self-improvement and self-discovery. There are certainly others. I had done work on myself before and been in and out of therapy, but for me, nothing could provide the tranquility I enjoyed after an Ayahuasca ceremony. I had never touched upon such raw opening of my heart or such a feeling of surrender and serenity. My discoveries were confirming that the emotional affects the physical in every way.

* * *

In January 2016 I went back to Kaiser for a follow-up MRI. Of course, I was hoping it would show that the tumor had shrunk since the MRI that was taken six months earlier. Devastatingly, it did not.

"It doesn't look like anything has changed," Dr. Takasugi said. "So, we need to take care of this."

"OK," I said tentatively, "but I want to give it a few more months."

I was greatly disappointed, but not discouraged. The tumor hadn't shrunk, but it hadn't grown either. Something inside me spoke: *Just keep going. You'll find the way. You'll succeed.* The process needed more time.

I shared with the doctor all the things I had been doing: the ozone infusions, raw foods, B-17 and vitamin C injections, and so on.

She was impressed.

"I, too, believe in a healthy lifestyle and alternative healing. However, we need to take it out, even though it's at an early stage. I recommend a mastectomy, followed by chemo and possibly radiation. I know that's not what you want to hear or what you want to do."

I liked Dr. Takasugi very much. Knowing that she had only my best interests at heart, and even though she was speaking to me quite bluntly, she spoke in a gentle and kind tone. I told her I was not ready for those steps, and left, promising to return in a few months.

I began to hear criticisms from a few friends when they learned I was not rushing into surgery and chemo.

"Are you crazy?" one friend said. "You're gambling with your life! Please listen to your doctor."

I knew that the people who said these things had good intentions and were just afraid for me. Clearly, they cared. I didn't tell them what was seriously occupying my thoughts— the lasting side effects that chemotherapy and radiation could have on me: a weakened immune system, loss of muscle sensation, permanent numbness, hair loss, nausea, skin problems, weight loss, and fatigue. I just refused to accept that kind of poison into my system.

* * *

Months later, in the summer of 2016, Shawn and I were especially eager to leave all my cancer-fighting activities behind, and go on our annual trip to visit my family in Croatia. It was such a pleasure to spend a few weeks with my parents in the small, quaint village where I was born. While we were there, we made jam from scratch. We picked about one hundred pounds of organic plums from the backyard, washed and pitted them, and then cooked them outdoors in a huge kettle over a fire. The jam had to be continuously stirred for six hours before it cooled and was transferred into canning jars. What fun we had! It reminded me of the delightful years I had growing up in the former Yugoslavia.

After ten days with my mother and my father, Shawn and I drove three hours to the Adriatic coast, to Split—for me, one of the most beautiful cities in the world. We were ready for some alone time, looking forward to a romantic getaway where we could lie on the beach, walk along the Riva boardwalk, and dine in cozy restaurants while looking out at the stunning sea.

We had brought my most recent MRI to show a radiologist colleague of mine in Split, as we wanted his opinion. He suggested that I have another MRI done in his office, which I did on the spot.

The next day, which happened to be July 4, Shawn and I waited anxiously for the results in a coffee shop next to the radiologist's office. It had been a whole year since my original diagnosis: a year of great sacrifices, cleansing, and turmoil. Waiting for Dr. Blago, I considered all the time and energy we had invested in overcoming this disease. Would our efforts pay off?

Dr. Blago arrived and sat down with us.

Without hesitation he said, "The tumor has definitely shrunk since the last MRI done in Los Angeles, and . . ."

Shawn and I both jumped from our seats and grabbed each other. We were overwhelmed with relief and deep gratitude. Tears of joy and happiness ran down our faces. We pulled away from each other to hear the rest of what Dr. Blago had to say.

"The MRI shows that the tumor looks extremely dark inside. This is very good because 'dark' means it's mostly dead. I also had another doctor in my practice look at it, and she agrees. I'm so glad to give you such good news."

Our hearts were overflowing with gratitude. It seemed our prayers had been answered.

CHAPTER 5

Facing Death

At the end of September, Shawn and I packed our yoga mats and clothes, and drove off to the desert for a yoga festival in beautiful Joshua Tree National Park. Each fall we attend Bhakti Fest, a five-day program where we immerse ourselves in yoga, personal growth workshops, meditation, and breathwork sessions, while enjoying great vegetarian food. We dance to a sacred form of music called Kirtan and celebrate ancient Indian traditions, some of which I am very familiar with from childhood. My father had sung several of those same Sanskrit songs to us as children, lovingly reminding me of my upbringing and connecting me to my heart. Bhakti Fest is always a delightful, uplifting environment, where we unplug and recharge our bodies and souls, an event we share with the energy of several thousand other attendees.

One early morning, after a strenuous yoga class under the hot desert sun, accompanied by live sacred music, I happily drifted into the shower, feeling grounded and at peace. My calm state of mind was suddenly disturbed when I felt what appeared to be a lump in my right armpit. The last thing I wanted to think about was cancer! I nervously told Shawn about it, and we reassured each other that it was probably just a swollen lymph node. Still, we agreed that it would be best for me to go to the doctor as soon as we returned home.

Back in Dr. Takasugi's office, I showed her where I had felt the lump. She examined the area and immediately said, "I need to biopsy this."

I had read somewhere that when you jab into something internal, it can spread; therefore, I did not want to have a biopsy. I told Dr. Takasugi that I wanted to wait a bit longer. She was not happy, as I was becoming a stubborn and challenging patient!

Three weeks later, I felt another lump right next to the first one. This one was larger—about the size of a hazelnut, and I knew for sure it hadn't been there before. Where had these lumps come from? I couldn't believe it. I was shocked. Now with two lumps and a knot of anxiety in my gut, there was no choice; I had to have a biopsy.

Days later, I was in the hospital having the procedure. It involved inserting a very thin needle into my swollen underarm to remove some sample tissues.

It wasn't long before I received a call from Dr. Takasugi. I literally held my breath as I braced myself for what she was going to say.

"Mrs. Clancy, I'm sorry. This isn't good news. You have a different kind of cancer now. It's called HER2, and it's very aggressive. It is already in your lymph nodes and therefore considered Stage 3. This means it's too late for surgery. We need to start you on chemotherapy right away."

The news came as another horrifying blow. The world seemed to crumble beneath me, and I don't even remember if I said a single word or just hung up the phone.

"Chemo? NO! I will *never* do chemo! I'd rather die than put that kind of poison into my body. I *can't* do chemo!" I screamed out at Shawn as I stood there, paralyzed, in our kitchen.

My husband was trying to hold me while I collapsed in tears and choking sobs. The petrifying anxiety of chemotherapy and its side effects were almost greater than the fear of cancer itself. How could I have had a "dead" tumor only a few months before, in July, but now have Stage 3 cancer, which is much more severe and threatening?

With my first diagnosis, I had decided to take full responsibility for getting this disease. To many people, it may sound unreasonable, even absurd, to explore the idea that inner psychological or emotional issues could be the root cause of cancer manifesting in the body. However, throughout my life I had never considered a victim consciousness to be part of my makeup. Therefore, I accepted that in some ways I had to be responsible for my health.

Only someone who has faced a cancer diagnosis can understand how devastating it is, and I am especially proud of how I chose to deal with it. I relentlessly attacked it from every plausible angle and tried to maintain a positive attitude.

My three Ayahuasca ceremonies, and all my energy during the previous year and a half, had been focused on not only learning *why* cancer had manifested, but also on getting rid of it at its source—both physically and emotionally.

I knew the inner work I had achieved and the incredible insights I had gained made space for my healing. In addition, I had detoxed in every possible way. I had diligently learned and practiced emotional release, self-forgiveness, and self-love—and consistently declared positive affirmations. To suddenly feel that none of it may have mattered, and that I wasn't done yet, was shocking and demoralizing.

The dark, ominous cloud I had kept at bay returned. While I could never completely shake some underlying fear during the past eighteen months, now it was overpowering. What is this cancer trying to tell me? Why did it have to come back? Was this going to be the end of my life's journey?

Shawn and I were traumatized once again. My husband wasn't just afraid; he was terrified, yet never showed it. For my sake, he managed a brave and confident demeanor. Only later did he confess his sense of unspeakable loss in imagining life without me, a vision that was unbearably painful.

Meditating helped us immensely. I was introduced to Transcendental Meditation at the age of ten back in Germany, and Shawn started TM shortly after we met. Since my father was a teacher of TM, my entire family meditated on a regular basis when I was growing up. Meditating supported me tremendously in keeping the fear at bay. Listening to different "I am" affirmations about health on YouTube helped me shift into a more positive state of mind as well. It took a lot of commitment and conscious effort to change my thoughts.

Sharing, accepting, and voicing my fears with Shawn whenever they would show up, helped me, too. He would hold me and be there for me whenever I would break down and cry. Having his support was critical during that time. Loved ones and friends would say how sorry they were, but hardly anyone asked how Shawn was. Cancer affected everyone in my family, especially my husband. He was going through his own emotional roller coaster without ever showing it, particularly after this second diagnosis.

When I was told that I had Stage 3 and that the cancer was in my lymph nodes, the anxiety and panic were dramatically worse than the first time. Having cancer in my defense mechanisms and immune system, and not in just one area of my breast, was terrifying and extremely serious. But being proactive by doing things that I thought would help me heal made the fear flare up less often.

Despite the doctor's bad news, I still believed the answers were to be found within. After my initial despair, I chose once again to take full responsibility for how I would handle this unexpected new diagnosis. As I began to process this unforeseen reality, I knew that this cancer had something more to teach me. It had returned for a reason. I was determined to find out what it was.

"Shawn, we need to go back to Bogotá," I said. "I have this strong feeling that the answers to this cancer are still inside me. My intuition is pulling me back toward Ayahuasca."

Mama Aya had connected me to my Higher Self, and apparently there was more to be revealed. I believed that this magical medicine would, once again, become the bridge that would lead me to what lay beneath and what needed to be brought to the surface. I felt strongly that "She" could help me discover the correct path to choose.

"We could go back and see Lluis," Shawn said, "but I was just speaking to my friend Russell, who told me about a woman here in L.A. She is a skilled facilitator with Ayahuasca. Why don't we meet with her first?"

"I don't know, Shawn," I replied. "I trust Lluis completely."

"Let's meet her and see how we feel. If we are not totally enthusiastic about her, we'll get on a plane," Shawn promised.

A few days later we were sitting at Café Gratitude, a couple of blocks from Venice Beach, with Russell and a lovely young woman named Briana. I had been skeptical about meeting her, not only because I had such faith in Lluis, but also because she was only thirty years old. Given my life experience, I wondered what someone that much younger than myself could possibly teach me. I believed that becoming an expert facilitator required a great deal of wisdom and maturity.

Briana and Russell were waiting at the restaurant when we arrived. The first moment I saw her, I felt her radiating awareness, beauty, and strength. She had a powerful, yet angelic presence, and I experienced an instant connection with her. As we spoke over lunch, I opened up to her with my story. She was tuned in, compassionate, and present. Even though I had just met her, I found myself trusting her in a way that was essential for these kinds of ceremonies.

Briana had grown up in Southern California, but went to the harsh and dangerous parts of the Amazon Jungle to find healing through Ayahuasca. She had lived through a number of rough years and was seeking answers regarding her life's path. She began her journey in Costa Rica, where she studied different plant medicines with the Secopai people from Ecuador.

She continued her training under a teacher from the Shipibo tribe, one of many indigenous people living in the Amazon Basin of Peru. The Shipibo people are deeply influenced by the power of plants, animals, and natural elements. Many of them become shamans or faith healers. This began Briana's personal journey with Ayahuasca.

"I experienced profound healing in Peru, so I decided to stay in South America," she said. "For ten years, I studied with several medicine teachers who had guided me in many different ceremonies, and trained me in various ways of healing with plants. At first, they were not keen to teach me since I was a woman. The medicine healed me from an eating disorder and severe depression. At times I had even considered suicide. I felt the plant medicine call me to study it and share this healing work."

Briana had also become a life coach and student of Neuro-Linguistic Programming (NLP). This is a program that works on the principle that everyone has the internal resources they need to make positive changes in their lives.

Like Lluis, Briana had obvious respect for the power of sacred plant medicine. She may have been young, but she quickly won me over. Shawn and I had agreed that we would not make any hasty decisions or engage her before consulting each other privately. After lunch, we thanked her for meeting us, said good-bye, and watched as she crossed the street to go to her car.

As Shawn and I turned to walk in the other direction, we looked at each other and knew without words that we both felt the same. We couldn't believe what had just occurred. Briana wasn't somebody we merely stumbled upon who happened to have access to Ayahuasca. This was a woman with tremendous commitment to this special gateway of healing. We knew she had a gift, and we found ourselves blessed to be in a receiving position. It seemed as if the Universe had arranged to bring us together.

Shawn and I smiled at each other, turned around, and ran toward her.

"Wait, Briana. We want you! We want you," we shouted to her.

Filled with joy, we agreed to set up a ceremony a few days later, on December 31, 2016.

There was no time to lose. My situation was urgent. I wasn't sure which scared me more: Stage 3 HER2 cancer or the thought of chemotherapy dripping into my veins. Because the cancer was in the lymph nodes, targeted chemotherapy was no longer an option. The chemo would invade my entire body—a brutal experience. Complications from chemotherapy can persist for years, compromising the immune system. It can create a loss of sensation in the limbs, which in my case was overly concerning because my right arm is vital in performing my AtlasProfilax work.

* * *

It was New Year's Eve, and instead of going to a party or out to dinner, Shawn and I were settled in a cozy, charming living room in a private home with Briana. We were eager to have her lead us in our Ayahuasca ceremony. In addition to Shawn and me, she had invited four other people to participate, all of whom we had never met. Briana had arrived hours ahead in order to prepare the space. She rearranged furniture and created an altar on the living room table with the sacred vine, crystals, wild tobacco leaves, sage, and feathers. Briana set a "healing mat" in the middle of the room, to be used later by anyone who wanted to receive energetic healing from others. She lit candles around the house, turned off the lights, and played Icaros softly. Her commitment to healing people was unwavering, and I felt such appreciation that she was right here in California.

She opened the ceremony with a prayer in Portuguese, singing in a beautiful, mellow tone, and then invited us each to state our intentions.

"Please show me what I need to do now. What else is there for me to learn from this experience? I need clear guidance," I conveyed to the group.

Shawn shared his intentions next: "I would like profound insights that will inspire me to awaken each day with trust, freedom, and more self-love."

We all received a shot of the mystical brew and lay down on our mats. As I felt the medicine expanding my consciousness and taking me to familiar places, I began to have extraordinary visions. I didn't feel sick at all this time. I distinctly saw myself standing in our bathroom in front of the large mirror. I looked at myself utterly naked, without a single hair on my body—no eyebrows, no eyelashes, completely bald. Moments passed when I heard a soft voice within: "Do you love yourself now? *Can* you love yourself like *this*?"

In Bogotá, my Ayahuasca visions had been focused on my self-perception. I had always been very hard on myself— judgmental even—and, as I mentioned previously, I had been habitually obsessed with my looks. To the outside world, I seemed quite confident, but the men in my life before Shawn constantly made me feel insufficient. From my first Ayahuasca experiences, I thought I had learned the importance of fully loving and appreciating my body. Seeing myself stripped down completely, as a hairless cancer patient, however, presented a far deeper level of acceptance that I had yet to achieve.

Standing in front of that mirror, I eventually heard my own voice in my mind, say, "*Yes! Yes, I can love myself like that.*" It felt as if I was wholly embracing myself, physically and emotionally, for the first time in my life.

That image slowly began to drift away, and in its place another one emerged. In this vision, not only was I hairless, but now also emaciated, no more than ninety pounds of skin and bones. The woman I had known as Jasna was hunched over, leaning on a cane, crippled by cancer, dying a slow, cruel death. It was the most foreboding and horrific sight I had ever seen.

I heard the voice again, this time asking, "Is this what you're afraid of?"

I didn't want to look. I turned away, but the voice was strict and insistent: "Look at it! Look at it! Look at your biggest fear." It felt as if an angel of death was yelling at me.

Unwillingly, I turned to look at the horrendous vision of a dying Jasna, and somehow, I acknowledged the truth. My whole body shivered as I faced my biggest fear and looked death straight in the eye.

"Yes! I am afraid of death. I am afraid that cancer and chemo will kill me!"

Time stood still when a soft voice, gently whispered, "That is not going to happen . . . Now, turn your head and look over here."

I was relieved to turn away from that ghastly vision. Slowly, I turned my head to the left and saw myself fully restored to health. I was smiling and happy, with cute short hair growing back. That's when I heard a loud, stern voice.

"You need to do chemo, and you need to do it *NOW!* Go to the doctor tomorrow and start right away. After two rounds of chemotherapy, your tumor will be completely gone. Chemo will kill all the cancer cells, and you will be fine."

Say what?!

Even though in an altered state, feeling One with the Universe, I was stunned.

Immediately after processing those words, I was drawn into a distinct vision of a young doctor, one I had not met before, standing in front of me as I sat in his office chair. This doctor had an amazed expression on his face as he said to me, "You're doing extremely well! Your tumor, which was the size of a tennis ball, is completely gone after just two rounds of chemotherapy. It's incredible! You are going to be fine."

I had one final, vivid vision that night. I was sitting by myself on the deck at the bow of a boat wearing a colorful two-piece bathing suit. I noted that I had very little hair on my head and saw my feet dangling over the water. I was looking out at the crystal-clear, deep blue ocean, with tears of joy rolling down my cheeks.

"I am cancer free! I did it!" I yelled to myself. I was filled with an overwhelming wave of gratitude and love for my life.

After that beautiful image, I felt drawn to lie upon the healing mat. The song that Briana was playing swept over me and seemed to pour into my soul. I felt my heart expanding.

That night, one of the women in attendance kneeled beside me. She laid one hand on my tumor, and the other on my stomach.

This woman, whom I had never met before, leaned over me and began to whisper very rapidly, over and over again, "You're well, you're well, you're well! You're healed, you're healed, you're healed! You're free, you're free, you're free!"

For about thirty minutes she administered her healing energy, continuously repeating those words softly and swiftly. I felt her message penetrate every cell of my body. Tears began to flow down my face, as I sat up and hugged her.

She then softly whispered such profound words: "As I was healing you, I was healing myself, too."

Soon after, Briana announced the closing of the ceremony, and I knew with great conviction what I had to do.

Two days later I was back at Kaiser for my first meeting with an oncologist assigned to me, named Dr. Ferreira. I told him I was ready for chemotherapy, and he looked utterly perplexed. He had reviewed my file and seen all the notes over the course of eighteen months about my resistance to standard Western medicine protocol.

He momentarily stuttered, "That's a very wise decision. I'll set you up to begin next week. You will do six rounds of chemo, three weeks apart."

Once I chose to do chemotherapy, I chose it powerfully and went all in. There was no doubt or second-guessing myself. I wasn't afraid of chemo poisoning any longer. This was the right time and the right decision at this stage on my cancer path. I was confident that this liquid drug would help me and that my body was strong enough to deal with its side effects.

I sat in the depressing chemo room for the first time with about twenty other patients. Over the course of six long hours, four big bags of toxic chemicals that I had feared so greatly were now slowly dripping into my veins.

Knowing I had to nourish my body, I'd brought a sixty-four-ounce bottle of freshly squeezed, organic green juice, along with some healthy snacks.

At the end of the session, I joyfully declared, "Yeah! One down, five more to go!"

Shawn was always at my side, and each day I had chemo, his oldest daughter, Paige, would take the day off work to be with me. Her sincere compassion and love touched me deeply. I felt so blessed that both Shawn's daughters, Paige and Maddy, were very supportive with their genuine love for me. Not having children of my own, the love I continue to have for my stepdaughters is incredibly deep and special.

My dear friend Lisa, who had recently finished chemotherapy, came to see me a few days before I started my treatments. She brought many gifts, including one large, beautiful designer bag. She hugged me compassionately, in a way that could only come from someone who had lived through the same experience.

"This is for you," she said, handing me the bag.

Reaching inside, I first pulled out a soft, sky-blue, cozy blanket. As I laid it out over my lap, I read the words embroidered on it: "Bear Hugs, Happy Hugs, Super Duper Hugs, Giant Hugs." I couldn't help but smile from ear to ear. I reached in again and pulled out a heating pad, as well as a variety of scarves and hats. Knowing that I would lose all of my hair soon, Lisa had thoughtfully brought two mannequin headstands topped with wigs as well. I was touched and moved to tears.

"Now, remember," she said, "I want you to picture all of those cancer cells being eaten up like Pac-Man. The chemo will gobble them all up!"

I did as she said, and pictured the yellow cartoonish mouth of my Chemo Pac-Man, chasing down each rapidly growing cancer cell one by one, chomping them up until they were all gone. I actively envisioned these little guys at every chemo session, and it made me feel happy and optimistic. At the same time, very unexpectedly, I began to develop an enormous appreciation for this chemo drug. *This is medicine, not poison. These chemicals will heal me*, I thought. Yes, it was harsh on the system, and yes, it killed good cells along with the bad.

But it had helped millions of people overcome cancer. For this, I felt enormous gratitude. I even daydreamed about the doctors in their lab coats and all of those researchers in their laboratories who had worked painstakingly for decades to create this treatment for cancer. There were so many people involved and committed to saving my life, as well as the lives of millions of others.

I directed my focus on appreciation, both inside and outside the medical world. All my family and friends, near and far, offered their love, prayers, and messages of healing. It was common to hear them say, "Let me know if there is anything I can do to help."

Shawn and I made a decision to not let these offers just pass us by, but to consciously accept and receive any contributions. This was contrary to my nature. I had a tough time receiving anything—compliments, gifts, or any kind of help. I had always been the *doer*, the *giver*. This was the image I had cultivated, and one that helped me maintain a feeling of control over my life. I liked being the one in charge. My default was to redirect attention away from myself, even when I was having a hard time and to shrug it off, saying, "Don't worry; I'm fine."

I had the typical cancer mentality: "I don't want to be a burden." This new bout of cancer, nonetheless, was teaching me that it was time to admit, "I'm not fine. I have frickin' cancer. I need to receive and allow people to give to me." What

I discovered was that I had a hard time receiving because I didn't have much self-love. Accepting and asking for help is self-love, and I needed to practice more receiving in order to heal. In that way, I was also allowing others the opportunity to support me and help me.

It had been two years since I had met Shawn, and I'd begun to trust him with my heart implicitly, but that was still not the same as self-love.

"Angel, healing happens in your heart, and part of self-love is learning how to receive," Shawn told me. "And in receiving, you are also giving. There are so many people who want the opportunity to participate in your healing."

I knew he was right. I tried to focus my attention on all the loving energy that was coming my way. I was learning to be a giver through being a receiver. In this positive flow, I would soon uncover the power and the gift of acknowledgment.

We created a project called "Food Angels," and Paige enthusiastically volunteered to become the facilitator. She knew that I would be in no shape to prepare food, and Shawn had his hands more than full, running his business and taking care of me. Paige contacted dozens of family members and friends. She set up a dinner rotation where local loved ones prepared home-cooked meals. As chemo inherently weakens the immune system, Paige emphasized how important it was to be scrupulous about washing the food, as well as their hands. For the "Angels" in other cities, Paige provided a list of our favorite restaurants, from which they ordered meals to be delivered. We took pictures of those delicious meals and sent them to the people who had lovingly and generously arranged for them. I actually found unbridled joy in expressing acknowledgment for all their kindness and consideration. In the circle of giving and receiving lies the gift of acknowledgment, and in deep gratitude, we thanked every individual for their loving contributions and the positive impact it had on me.

When I informed Lluis that I was going to do chemo, he supported me in that decision, and even told me that Ayahuasca could help me during chemotherapy. He said that it boosts the red blood cells and kills parasites. He warned me, however, not to take Ayahuasca right after a treatment, but to wait at least a week.

When I told my family in Croatia about my new diagnosis and chemo treatment plan, it led to another, totally unexpected gift from cancer: my mother immediately offered to come from Croatia, and my sister announced she was flying in from Canada. They were eager to help me in whatever way they could. When I told them about all of the positive visions I'd seen in my journeys with Lluis and Briana, they said that they were excited to try Ayahuasca along with me.

Would they really be ready to try this powerful, yet radical, gateway to healing for themselves?

CHAPTER 6

Family Journey

One evening, about a week after my second round of chemo, I was sitting on a chair in our bathroom, my back to the mirror. Shawn was clipping away with the scissors, cutting my hair shorter and shorter. Pink Floyd's *Dark Side of the Moon* was playing in the background. As my hair was dropping to the floor, I thought about the time I had visited a yoga ashram in India in 2001, when I'd considered shaving my head as a fashion statement.

This time, however, the bold look was not a choice, just inevitable. I refused to let my hair loss bring me down.

"Great! No more bad hair days. No more worries about styling, coloring, or blow drying. We'll save tons of money on hairdressers!" I jokingly said to my husband.

When Shawn had finished his handiwork with the electric trimmer, I turned around hesitantly to look at myself in the mirror. To my surprise, I thought my buzz cut looked downright badass, and I felt strangely liberated.

"It looks cool!" I said. "Now, let's shave it all off."

"Really? Now?" My husband was surprised.

"Yes, let's do it. It's going to fall out soon, and I planned on shaving it all off anyway."

I had begun waking up in the mornings to more and more of my hair on the pillow, in addition to what was falling out in the shower.

The bag of colorful scarves and wigs my friend Lisa had given me still sat in my room. Nonetheless, I was going to own my temporary hairless condition just as I owned my entire cancer experience. Once or twice I tried wearing a wig, but it was quite itchy. A few times I tried wrapping a pretty scarf around my head, but covering up just wasn't in my nature. Besides, losing my hair was the least of my problems!

Life goes on, and things happen—even when going through a major health crisis, like cancer. Not only was I barely keeping it together trying to survive this new challenge, but I also had to deal with the unexpected that life can throw at us.

Days after being diagnosed with Stage 3 cancer, we received an early-morning knock on our front door. To our surprise,

Shawn was served with a subpoena. His ex-wife had decided to take him back to court for additional alimony payments. This came as a shock, because he had fulfilled all obligations in their marital settlement agreement. Having already spent tens of thousands of dollars on alternative treatments, and with my not having worked for over a year, our financial resources were now uncomfortably scarce.

I can't even begin to describe the stress that came with the legal process that we were forced to go through. It was not only erroneous, but it was also devastating. I was weak, tired, hairless, and on the verge of sheer panic at a time when I couldn't afford to be overwhelmed with anxiety. Looking back now, between my fear of dying from this second cancer diagnosis, the chemo, the lawyers and lawsuit, and the accumulated financial and emotional burdens, those months were by far the worst and most difficult in my entire life.

When Shawn had finished shaving my head, I looked in the mirror again and felt like a new person. I saw a warrior woman—the most raw and natural version of myself.

It wasn't sad. In fact, it was an empowering, yet vulnerable feeling when I ran my hands over the soft skin of my naked scalp for the first time. *Now when I go out, everyone will know,* I thought. *Look at me. I have cancer. And, I'm not hiding it.* It gave me a sense of freedom.

Shawn likes to refer to his bald head as a "styling choice" and pulls it off without any problem. Once we had matching "haircuts," it was fun taking selfies together. When we went out, some people would say, "Oh, that's so sweet. Your husband shaved his head to support you." We'd just nod and smile, letting them think that Shawn had actually done that. (And, of course, he would have!)

When Paige first saw me afterward, she asked, "Aw! Did you cry when Dad shaved your head?"

"Nope," I smiled. "Not at all. I chose it because it was bound to happen. This way, it gives me a sense of control. Now I can look forward to my hair growing back. I've heard it might even come back curly. How cool would that be?"

Having all the love, strength, and nurturing I needed from Shawn, his daughters, my family, and my close friends, I didn't feel the need to attend any cancer support groups. I did go to one workshop in order to learn how to pencil in my almost-gone eyebrows. Having no hair was one thing, but having no eyebrows and looking like an alien was quite another. The feeling at the workshop was a little heavy for me, though. When I walked in, I felt there was a silent acknowledgment of the inner strength we each were forced to develop, but among the fifteen women there, some were predominantly radiating fear and sadness. The environment didn't really resonate with me, so I left early. My heart went out to them, and I hoped they would each find their own empowering path.

Although chemo made me lose my hair, as it does for most people, overall, I was very fortunate that the side effects were not as horrific as I thought they would be. I felt a bit nauseated, but never to the point of throwing up. Without a doubt, I believed that my attitude and efforts to cleanse my body over the previous year and a half were the reasons chemo wasn't taking as significant a toll on my system as it could have. My body was well prepared for this heavy-duty cocktail. The worst part was the terrible, awful taste of metal in my mouth. No matter what I tried, I couldn't get rid of it. Everything tasted like metal, and I hated it.

I did get tired more easily and slept far more than usual. Also, my skin became extraordinarily sensitive. Sunbathing, which I absolutely love to do, was dangerous during chemo. One of the reasons I had moved to L.A. was to enjoy the year-round California sunshine. Staying away from it was tough for me.

Surprisingly, a couple of weeks after each chemotherapy session I felt well enough for some moderate exercise. I enjoyed walking and sometimes jogging on the beach, covering myself with long sleeves and a wide-brimmed hat, of course. Frequently, I even went to the gym. Whenever in public, however, I was especially careful to use hand sanitizer regularly. With my weakened immune system, I was at extremely high risk for bacterial infections and was concerned about catching random germs in public.

The nurses in the chemo room made the experience as uplifting as could be. Each and every one of them was open-hearted, playful, encouraging, tireless, and simply wonderful. We were assigned a different nurse each time and learned this was intentional, so that we would not become emotionally attached to a single caregiver. (And perhaps it was also a protection for them not to become overly attached to us either.)

After the second round of chemo, I showed up for an appointment with my new oncologist, Dr. Ferreira, who was monitoring my progress.

"You're doing extremely well!" he said after he'd examined me. "I can't even feel your tumor anymore. It was the size of a tennis ball, and it's already completely gone after just two rounds of chemotherapy. That's incredible! You are going to be fine."

Shawn was driving us home when I suddenly cried out, "*Oh my God!*"

I had remembered something of great significance! I silently reviewed what had just happened with Dr. Ferreira, and, in a blinding flash, realized that *this was exactly the vision I had seen two months earlier during my Ayahuasca journey with Briana!* His words were precisely the same, and so were our positions in the room. I was sitting, he was standing, and his mannerisms, gestures, tone of voice, and expression were identical to what I had seen. I'd been given a vision into the future, and here I was experiencing it in real time. Shawn and I had both witnessed a miracle! I was choked up with tears over this profound occurrence.

I still needed to complete all six rounds of chemo even though, just as I was shown, the first two rounds had dissolved the entire 3.4-inch tumor. Feeling so uplifted from my progress and from experiencing the truth of my Ayahuasca visions, I went forward with the last four treatments with great confidence.

I realized that all my fears of chemotherapy where exaggerated and were not nearly as bad as I had anticipated. My mind imagined it to be far worse than it really was. Talking to my friend Lisa, who had finished her chemo treatments just a couple of months earlier, helped ease a lot of my anxiety. I never got sick, although each treatment made me consistently more tired. And now that my two-year journey is over I can definitely say that I have not one permanent side effect from chemo.

My sister and mother had promised to come and support me during my chemotherapy phase and arrived at the midway point, after my third round. They were ready to offer me all the bolstering I needed, as well as to join us in a family Ayahuasca gathering. Being very intrigued by what I had gained in my previous ceremonies, they were brave enough to try it for themselves. Each one of us carries pain from the past, as individuals and as families. Plus, I wasn't the only one suffering from my cancer; my whole family constantly worried about me and therefore suffered along with me.

Little did we know that our being together as a family during that ceremony would bring healing to each of us and even change the dynamics of all of our relationships. Through working with this mysterious plant medicine, we discovered how we had held on to different patterns that influenced our behaviors. We never fought with one another, but we gained insights into how certain events in our lives continued to trigger behaviors that did not serve us.

We organized a private family ceremony with Shawn, my mother, my sister Zana, my brother Vladimir, Paige, and her girlfriend Kelsey. This time, Briana wanted to invite people from her Aya community who played live music—a guitar player who had an angelic voice, a master of didgeridoo (a four-foot wooden drone pipe), a drummer, and a flute player—and a co-facilitator to assist people whenever they needed help. We enthusiastically agreed to have her ensemble join us. As she always did, Briana created a beautiful ceremonial space. She covered the TV with a charming print curtain and arranged Indian hawk feathers, cougar furs, sheep skin, candles, and handmade leaf fans strategically throughout the room. Next to each of our mats, she placed the all-important, cheerful, multicolored buckets that we might need during our experiences.

"The bucket is your best friend tonight," she said with a smile.

Out of respect for the elderly, my mother was the first to be invited to receive the magical brew. She was seventy-four years old at the time.

As Briana poured her the first shot, we could hear my mother whisper in broken English, "Not too little."

The rest of us chuckled. We admired my mother's courage. She wasn't willing to participate less than anyone else. On the contrary, she was like a gallant queen ready to lead her people into battle.

My mother was born in a small village in the southern part of former Yugoslavia in 1942, amid the chaos of World War II. Everyone in Europe was suffering from the effects of that war—not only the physical danger of being bombed or taken prisoner, but, in the case of people who lived in her village, inescapable poverty as well. My mother was lying between my sister and me as we started to feel the effects of the medicine. Briana and her co-facilitator were thoughtfully watching over her throughout the night.

I leaned toward her and whispered, "Are you okay, Mom? Do you feel sick?"

"No, I am fine. I don't feel sick at all. But I need to go within now," she said with a smile, kissing me on the forehead.

As she was soaring in the mysterious realm of the medicine, my mother was taken back to her time as an infant. She saw that she was terribly hungry—literally starving. Her mother had no breast milk. My mom was the third child, and her parents had accepted the inevitable tragedy that this baby girl would die, just as other babies in their village had. She saw herself as a baby who couldn't stop crying from hunger, a heartbreaking situation that lasted for many months.

My mother heard her own voice in her mind, *This child is so hungry, so desperately hungry. Oh my God! She is starving!* She then heard her Highest Self telling her, *This baby needs love. Give her some love.*

Who can love a starving, crying baby like this? she responded. *I can't love this baby. I usually love babies, but I don't want to love this one. I don't know why, but I have no feelings for this child.*

The voice of Mama Aya and the voice of my mother went back and forth, with Aya gently urging her, *Love this baby. Embrace this baby. She needs your love.* My mother refused, not understanding why she couldn't. Eventually she agreed to hold the baby, but all she saw was a sickly, starving, dying infant. For some reason, her heart could not feel compassion.

When my mother came out of her journey, she was astonished. Never had she realized how close she had come to dying during the war. She had not comprehended how hard her parents had to work to keep themselves and their children alive during such desperate times. Like everyone else in their village, they'd manually harvested corn and wheat on their small farms.

Farmers in former Yugoslavia had to give almost all their crop yields over to the Communist government to be shared with the whole country. Even though they grew their own food, they themselves were deprived. It was common during those years for village parents to lose infants and young children to hunger. Only after this insight did my mother realize just how close she had come to suffering that same terrible fate.

That night, Vladimir, Zana, and I gained an entirely new understanding of our mother. All her life she had been a compulsive eater, constantly grabbing something to put into her mouth. Unknowingly, she had a persistent fear of hunger—maybe there won't be enough food to eat! It was a deep-seated fear of starvation, born of her own terrible hunger in infancy. Luckily, her metabolism was incredibly fast, and she never gained weight no matter how much she overate.

At last, our mother understood the root cause of this hunger—where it came from, and why it was never satisfied. My grandparents had expected their baby girl to die and withheld love as a way to protect their hearts. Our mother had been starving—as a baby, for food, and as an adult, for the affection that she had been denied in infancy. Even though her parents showered her with love later, the memory of that trauma became part of her psyche.

The next morning, after breakfast, Briana organized an integration meeting. We formed a circle, going around one at a time, sharing as much of our visions as was comfortable. Briana encouraged us to contemplate our insights, which would lead to greater understanding and healing. Incorporating our new discoveries and self-knowledge back into our day-to-day lives and working through what we had released were necessary components to maximize our Ayahuasca experience. With Briana's guidance, my mother knew that the best way to heal was to imagine holding herself as a newborn—embracing her, hugging her, kissing her, and showering her with the love she deserved and needed, but had never received.

During integration, Mom shared with us her feeling of Oneness with the Universe and a sense that she had arrived home at last.

"I don't know how else to explain it, but it felt like I could literally talk to God." She was overwhelmed with gratitude as tears of joy were flowing down her face. "I was exploring levels of consciousness I didn't know existed," she told us. "I was able to tap into memories I never knew were there and open my heart to self-love so I could heal. It was a complete sense of knowingness. I feel truly blessed and so fortunate to have had this profound experience at my age." She thanked Briana profusely.

Not until she saw herself as a starving, unloved newborn, did she recognize that she had never really loved herself, even as an adult. It was a dark, tough road for her to travel that finally allowed her access to self-love and a compelling sense of rebirth. Vladimir, Zana, and I told her what a wonderful, caring mother she was. Finally, in that moment, she was able to truly hear and accept what we were saying. I shared my self-love practice with her, so she, too, began to pause every time she would see herself in the mirror and was sure to say something nice to her reflection. She created her own ritual of appreciating her healthy body as a lovely vessel, taking care of herself much more than before, being proud of herself, and simply focusing on the things she appreciates in her life.

In that same ceremony, she also saw how much guilt she carried about not having been a good mother to her children, especially to me, as the eldest. I was born when she was only twenty-one, while she was working full-time and still going to college. At twenty-five, she and my father moved to Germany for better opportunities and a higher standard of living. Life was hard for them, and we were extremely poor during those first few years. Neither of them spoke German, and they worked factory jobs that paid little.

In some ways, our family pattern had repeated itself. Due to the restrictive nature of the war, my mother's parents had been unable to give her what she needed. A generation later, my mother was also unable to provide her daughters the love and attention she knew they needed. Parents in survival mode don't have the energy or awareness for anything more than just getting by. That night, my mom understood this all-pervasive guilt and saw how it was not serving her. From there, she was able to take the first steps toward releasing it. In this way and more, her Ayahuasca experience was life altering.

That day after our gathering, my mom and I were sitting on the living room couch.

She began to apologize, "Jasna, I am so sorry I didn't give you the love and attention I should have when you were a child. I neglected you completely! I was never there for you." She was crying, sounding heartbroken. "It's so clear to me now. Your father and I just did what we had to do to survive. We didn't know any better. Can you please forgive me for not being there for you?"

I felt deeply moved.

"There's nothing to forgive, Mom. I love you. It's okay."

"No, I need to hear you say that you forgive me," she begged.

"Yes, Mom, I forgive you, wholeheartedly."

She reached out her arms, and we held one another and cried.

I had felt very close to my mother before this journey, but afterwards something had shifted, and now we have an even deeper connection. The subtle, underlying guilt and shame that she carried throughout most of our past interactions were now gone. She no longer asked repeatedly, "Do you need anything? Can I do something for you?" Ever since her vision, she is much freer in her affection towards us all, and we can feel her beautiful, nourishing love washing over us every time we communicate. Ayahuasca had opened an opportunity for forgiveness and healing for all of us.

My mother had rediscovered herself at the age of seventy-four. The medicine took her to the root of her problem with food and her daily anxiety. With her new focus on self-appreciation, she lives with greater awareness and peace of mind.

"I am finally starting to fall in love with myself," she told me, with a bit of awe in her voice. "I am an entirely different person after *one* Ayahuasca journey."

My mother wasn't the only one who gained a new understanding of her past and what she needed to heal. My brother, sister, and I also discovered things about our lifelong patterns of interacting with one another that had held us back from developing closer relationships.

For example, in Zana's visions, she saw how she had always bickered with Vladimir. It wasn't anything serious, but a low-level tension was present every time they'd visit each other. She began to see that subconsciously she had taken her frustrations about men out on Vladimir—the youngest in the family and the only male she thought she could "manage."

Our father had been an authoritative figure, and between his overpowering presence and her having endured a bad marriage with a controlling husband, Zana had soured on men most of her life. She was surprised to realize how she had used Vladimir as a kind of whipping boy for her considerable frustrations with men. This new understanding led to a beautiful, open conversation between them, and she was able to apologize. Ever since, they are much closer; they connect on a deeper level and have a wonderful relationship.

Personally, I discovered critical things about my early years that had an almost eerie similarity to what my mother had found in her journey. My intention that night was to discover whether there was anything from my childhood that I needed to heal. What was this aggressive cancer trying to tell me?

In my previous journeys with Lluis, I had let go of all the pain and resentment I had toward my former boyfriends. With this new bout of cancer, I knew more healing was required, and I sensed there was something from my early life that I had not yet identified. In fact, my first years were very difficult, and I wondered what memories I had buried that might be blocking me from my full healing.

That night, I saw an image of myself as a very sad little girl. When I was five years old, my parents left unexpectedly and were gone for a couple of months, looking for better job opportunities in Cologne, Germany. Croatia was still part of the republic of Yugoslavia under Communist rule, and good-paying jobs were scarce. It was a bold and somewhat risky move because they did not speak the language and had to start from scratch.

My sister and I stayed with my grandparents, who lived on a farm in a small village in a remote area of Croatia. It was a simple, old-fashioned life. I loved my grandparents very much, but I missed my parents terribly. I was too young to understand why they had gone away and did not understand the concept of time well enough to know when they were coming back. Every day they were absent felt like forever.

There I was, every afternoon, waiting excitedly for the mailman to ring his bicycle bell. It meant there was mail for us—and possibly a letter from our parents!

One day when I heard his bell, I rushed towards the front gate of the house to get the mail. In my haste, I ran into the edge of the iron gate so hard that I cut my head open and was bleeding. To this day, I still have a scar high on the left side of my forehead.

I needed medical attention, and not wanting to frighten me, my grandfather enthusiastically said that he was going to take me to my aunt's house. My grandparents knew I loved to go there, and they told me that she would take care of my head. He set me sideways on the bar of his bicycle and began to ride down the road. But instead of taking me to my aunt's house, he made a detour to the doctor's office in the village. I was very upset, even outraged, that he had lied to me, yet I never expressed this or showed it in any way. It would have been very disrespectful to argue with an elder during those times in Yugoslavia. For the first time in my young life, I felt deeply betrayed, and by two people I loved and trusted the most: my grandparents.

The memory of that little white lie at five years old was burned into me. It taught me a lesson that I'd latched onto for my entire life . . . until this insightful vision. The moment I realized I had been lied to, I created a belief that it was OK to hide or manipulate information to protect people's feelings. Or, depending on the situation, to get them to do what I thought might be best for them.

Once the medicine had opened my eyes, I saw that throughout my life I had taken this behavior to the extreme. I had a pattern of manipulating conversations to avoid hurting other people's feelings. I might say to my sister, "You can tell Mom this part of what I'm telling you, but not that part." My sister would say, "Why don't you tell her the whole truth?" Regardless, as her big sister, she would always do as I asked.

Once again this powerful plant expanded my awareness and allowed me to identify where I felt betrayed for the first time in my life. It was amazing to me that this one otherwise small event from my early childhood had fundamentally shaped the way I managed—and mismanaged—so many of my relationships.

Painfully, I saw that in many ways I had become inauthentic. I finally understood how being inauthentic had kept my heart sealed shut and deprived me of my full self-expression.

In order to further protect myself, I'd learned to put limits on how closely I permitted people to know me, to ensure their potential lies could never hurt me again. Of course, that didn't work the way I had hoped. Life has a way of imposing on us the things we intend to avoid.

In that same journey another vision emerged, this one from when I was six. Moving to Germany, I was put into first grade without knowing how to speak or write German. Since I couldn't communicate, I didn't have any friends, and I couldn't express myself while at school. When the teacher asked me a question, I sat there blankly, unable to comprehend what she was saying. My parents couldn't help me with my homework either, since they too, did not yet speak the language. I saw myself sitting in school, feeling isolated and alone. Even at home, my parents had no time for me. Both of them were still working in a factory on the assembly line during the day, and my father had a second job at night loading trucks. Feeling alone and hopeless, those early years were an ongoing struggle for me—not exactly the life of a free-spirited child.

In every revisitation of my early childhood throughout that evening, I saw myself as a lonely child who never cried, but also as one who never smiled. Even at an early age, I was aware of the strong prejudice against foreigners in Germany. In the 1970s, Germany was taking in many Turkish and Yugoslavian immigrants, who all faced harsh discrimination. Most Germans hated "guest workers." Many times we heard children shout as they saw some Turkish people walking by, "Filthy foreigner! Go home!" I couldn't help but feel I might be one of those undesirables.

I had many different visions from my childhood that night, but the most intense one took me back to a sunny afternoon when I was nine years old. My mother told me to take Zana, who was seven, and two-year-old Vladimir, who had been born in Germany, to the playground a few blocks away. I was in charge of both of my younger siblings and took my job very seriously. My mother instructed Zana to listen to me, and with my parents out of the house so often, I ended up bossing her around quite frequently.

Back in Yugoslavia, it was entirely reasonable for children our age to roam around independently and unsupervised all day long. But this was Cologne, a big city with busy streets and heavy traffic. I walked my siblings to the playground, where we all started to play. We were having a lot of fun building a castle in a sandbox with a few other children. Before long, I noticed that Vladimir wasn't in the sandbox anymore. I looked around but didn't see him. My heart began racing like crazy. Our brother was gone! I was terrified. I ran to each area of the playground and couldn't find him.

Petrified, I ran through the open gate of the playground to the street, looking in every possible direction. I didn't see our baby brother anywhere. Zana was just following me around, not grasping the seriousness of the situation and certainly not concerned. After all, I was the older sister who took care of everything.

During this vision, I relived the desperate panic of losing my brother. Buried deep inside, it had remained in every cell of my body all these years! It was a traumatic memory that left me ice cold, tormented by the thought that something unspeakable might have happened to him and it would have been all my fault.

As I stood outside the playground with Zana next to me, I faced the busy double-lane intersection with traffic zooming by in opposite directions. Where would I even start looking for him? I felt weak, as if I might pass out. *There is no way I will find him. These streets are so busy! He could have gone in any direction! What if a car hit him?* I thought, standing there frozen in place. All of a sudden, across the street I noticed an older gentleman about a block away, walking hand in hand with a little blond boy.

As they came closer, the relief I felt as I recognized Vladimir was indescribable. I just wanted to collapse.

"I noticed you all playing in the sandbox earlier," the kindly man explained. "When I left the park, I saw him a couple of blocks away walking all by himself. I don't know how he could have crossed this busy street all alone without being run over!"

I can't even remember what I said. My mind was racing. All I could think was, *Thank you, dear God. Thank you, God!* Clutching Vladimir's hand very tightly, I led us back to our apartment. It took me hours to calm down. I instructed my sister not to tell anyone about this incident, since I felt so guilty for not watching him closely enough. Our parents never found out about it until many years later. When they did, they were shocked and relieved.

Reliving these traumatic episodes kindled a newly identified sense of anger within me toward my parents. How could they have put me in that situation? Cologne was not a small village. It was a large city, where anything could happen! How could they have given me the burden of such an adult responsibility when I was just a little girl?

The moment that anger surfaced, I heard a voice call out to me, "You have seen how hard it was for you. Now let's see how hard it was for your parents during those years."

Immediately, an image appeared showing my father, utterly exhausted, working two jobs to keep the roof over our heads and food in our bellies. One day, tired of being discriminated against and dealing with the endless name-calling, he lost his temper and punched a coworker in the face. He got fired on the spot.

My mother was still working long hours in a beer factory, even though she was pregnant with my brother and already had two little girls. I remember her being constantly sick. It suddenly became clear, *No wonder they didn't have time for me.* What hardship it was! My heart filled instantly with compassion for them. They were young school teachers from Yugoslavia, in their mid-twenties, adjusting to a new country and a new language, coping with prejudice, all the while trying to care for a growing family. When I saw this from their perspective, I came to realize that my parents had done everything they could to build a better life for us. I suddenly knew, *there was nothing to forgive.* All I felt was deep love for them.

My father had never shared any of these incidents with us. He had never once complained about the discrimination he'd suffered—not even to my mother—nor did he complain about having had to work in such difficult circumstances.

I was very proud of my father for how he had improved his situation in such a short time. In only three years, he learned German well enough to get hired as a physical education teacher at a high school. He also earned a third-degree black belt in karate. Shortly after that, he opened a karate studio in Cologne. Due to his success with the studio and landing a well-paying job as a teacher, he was able to move us to an upscale neighborhood. My discontented childhood was then replaced by the best childhood anyone could wish for. I had many new friends, spoke absolutely perfect German, and became one of the most popular girls throughout my remaining school years. I found my smile again.

All of this happened within four years after leaving the former Yugoslavia! A decade later, my father even returned to college and became a doctor of naturopathy.

The day after our ceremony, I couldn't wait to have a Skype call with my father and ask him about everything I had seen. He was very curious and enjoyed hearing all about our Aya experiences.

"Dad, I never understood all that you and Mom went through when we were little," I said to him. "Now I see how hard it was for you both. I am so proud of you for the life you made for yourself and for our family. You set an amazing example in overcoming any and all obstacles and how to move forward building a life in a new place."

"I don't even think about it anymore," he replied. "It's ancient history. I hope you are free of it too."

Just as my mother had seen herself as an unloved, hungry baby during World War II, in my visions that night, I was made aware that as a little child I lacked much-needed love. While I also gained insight into my parents' enormous efforts to survive and then thrive, I was still guided in my visions to hold little Jasna, hug her, and tell her all was well. I envisioned my mother cuddling, kissing, and embracing me. I knew she loved me, and always had.

In that state of higher consciousness, accessing regions of the brain where childhood trauma resides and bringing awareness to the source, I was able to release more emotional scars that I had not been aware of. The medicine allowed me to have empathy for my younger self who suffered those childhood experiences, and I was able to nourish my inner wounded child. When my mother had told me long ago that she felt very guilty for not being there for me, I didn't think I had been holding a grudge. But the pain was nonetheless there—until I let it go that night. I'd had no idea that my past had affected me so deeply for so long. I had to face the darkness within to release painful memories. This was a road I had to walk alone.

CHAPTER 7

No Regrets

In June 2017, two months after completing all six rounds of chemotherapy, I had a follow-up appointment with Dr. Takasugi. She arranged for an ultrasound, and Shawn and I were hopeful that she would send us off with news that I was completely finished with my cancer treatments.

That was not meant to be.

"The tumor is gone, but there is some calcification left in the breast," she explained. "This is a problem, because the calcification will continue to show up on mammograms, and the radiologist won't be able to tell the difference between the calcification and a potentially malignant tumor."

Here she stopped to take a deep breath.

"I know this is not what you want to hear, Mrs. Clancy, but under the circumstances a lumpectomy is not a viable option. That tumor was big—3.4 inches—and the leftover calcification is now lined up in a long row in your breast. We need to do a mastectomy."

I couldn't accept what she was saying. In my heart, I knew my body was free of any cancer cells. There was no doubt in my mind. Seeing my unhappy expression, she continued to present the situation in a more positive light.

"This won't be as bad as you think," she continued. "Since you have had implants before, you will only need one surgery for both the mastectomy and the reconstruction, instead of two separate surgeries. And we won't have to worry about any future mammograms that might look suspicious. I will also have to remove some lymph nodes. This is standard procedure to ensure there are no remaining cancer cells."

I felt so devastated by what she was saying that I didn't even respond. My awareness collapsed into one thought: *a mastectomy is amputation!*

Despite Dr. Takasugi's reassurances about the tumor being gone, I wasn't ready to cope with the trauma of losing my breast, even though I would need only one operation instead of two. I had already undergone two breast surgeries for augmentation, and a third surgery to correct a botched implant job. How many more surgeries would I have to endure?

And besides, my breast represents a sacred feminine part of me. I imagined that losing it was going to rob me of my femininity, just as I was getting in touch with that part of myself. The idea that it would be cut off was nothing short of a nightmare. A familiar deep despair wrapped itself around me.

This was yet another significant decision I had to make, one that would have permanent consequences. Once more, I trusted that Ayahuasca would take me to the infinite place within me, where in the absence of resistance, I would become aware of the best path for me. That week we organized another ceremony with Briana. My intention, of course, was to find out whether the mastectomy was absolutely necessary.

During this journey I lay there crying. Gut-wrenching tears flooded forth. I was not only weeping, I was mourning. *I don't want to lose my breast! This will be much worse than chemo. I don't want to do this!* I repeated terrifyingly in my mind while my hand protectively covered my chest. *I don't want to cut off my breast. I don't want to be butchered!*

Gradually, as I dove deeper into my consciousness, I heard a gentle, caring voice, and as odd as it seems, I heard it coming from my right breast.

"It's going to be okay."

I felt consoled as the voice continued, "It's not going to be a big deal. If I'm okay with it, you should be okay with it, too. I am a small price to pay for the amazing life you're about to have. Let me go with love . . . *release me* . . . just release me completely."

A sense of astonishment washed over me. My right breast was talking to me and comforting me. I thought, *That's one smart boob!* Now, with both hands covering my right breast, I started accepting the idea of letting go. I envisioned my breast slowly drifting and fading away into the distance as I was saying good-bye.

Forgive me for abusing you with three surgeries. I love you, and I thank you for helping me let go. Yes, it will all be okay!

Before this insight, I also had great concern over the removal of some of my lymph nodes. Removing them from that area could damage the feeling and sensation in my right hand, which I require when working on patients who come for the AtlasProfilax treatment. However, I came out of the journey with absolute certainty that surgery was the right path for me. My fear was gone, and I was sure everything would be fine.

A few days later, I sat in Dr. Takasugi's office.

With my newfound confidence I stated, "OK, I will have the surgery."

She smiled at me, relieved that I'd decided to follow her advice.

"You will have peace of mind now, and frankly, so will I," she said.

Dr. Takasugi explained in more detail what would be involved. She reiterated that having an existing implant would enable her to simply remove the necessary breast tissue, and then the plastic surgeon, Dr. Klausmeyer, would swap out the old implant for a new one.

I thought of my friend Lisa who had undergone a double mastectomy. She had shared with me that her reconstructed breasts looked better than her original ones, reassuring me that I would be happy with the results of my surgery as well.

Two weeks later, on June 19th, I was admitted to the hospital for my mastectomy and reconstructive surgery. Shawn, Paige, Kelsey, and Maddy were all with me. Dr. Takasugi greeted us warmly. Her compassionate demeanor over the past two years had cultivated in me a genuine trust in her.

"I want to thank you in advance for doing a great job with my surgery," I sincerely expressed to her from my hospital bed. "You have been so committed to my health, and you've been so patient with me for two years."

Dr. Takasugi tried to suppress a little smile, but without much success. She was very touched.

"I also want to acknowledge you for all of the women you have helped and for all the hard work and the sacrifices you and your family must have made in order for you to become such a wonderful surgeon."

She grabbed my hand as I was wheeled into the operating room.

Dr. Takasugi had planned to remove four lymph nodes, but she ended up having to remove six because they were too close together. When I woke from surgery, I felt a bit drowsy but good overall. With Shawn by my side, we spent the night at the hospital.

Once home, I recovered quickly. I never felt *any* pain, and I didn't have to take a single painkiller—no Tylenol, no Advil, no nothing! And, even though I had a drainage tube coming out of my chest for five days, there was no bruising. My body was in an accelerated healing mode. I was consuming a large number of vitamins and natural supplements, as well as Arnica pills every two hours, and drinking liquid collagen daily. I had four colonics over the next couple of weeks to flush out the anesthesia drugs from my system as quickly as possible. This healing regimen was based on my own holistic background and knowledge of how important it is to rebuild the immune system. Any form of surgery causes trauma and a shock to the body, and I believe the supplements and good nutrition helped me immensely in my recovery.

It was three days after surgery, when Dr. Takasugi called.

"Mrs. Clancy, the lab results came back, and I have some great news," she said in an upbeat voice. "We could not find *one* single cancer cell anywhere! Not in the breast tissue *or* in the lymph nodes! This is very rare. Usually, there are some cancer cells left. If that had been the case, you would have needed radiation. Not one cancer cell!"

"I feel like crying," I said to her.

"Me too!" she said lovingly. "I believe a lot of it had to do with your great positive attitude and taking such good care of your body. You really cleansed and nourished it. Now you'll probably ask, 'Why did we have to remove the whole breast, then?' Well, we couldn't know for sure if there were any cancer cells left until we did."

She then said encouragingly, "You will now have peace of mind."

As I hung up the phone, Shawn and I embraced and broke down in tears.

"I've been holding my breath for two years," my husband sighed. "Now, I can breathe again."

Only eight days after my surgery, I was lying at the pool in a bikini. Both Dr. Takasugi and Dr. Klausmeyer had done a fantastic job. My breast looked amazing. No one would have been able to tell that I'd just had major surgery!

* * *

Now that I was healed and cancer-free, we had to celebrate. Five weeks later, in July, our entire family on both sides, along with a dozen of our closest friends from America and Canada, all flew to Split, Croatia, to celebrate LIFE with me. We rented a huge yacht with nineteen cabins to host thirty-eight people. We cruised along the Adriatic coastline, anchoring in different secluded coves each day to swim in the sparkling blue sea. Stopping each evening at one of the many stunning Croatian islands, we would explore and enjoy the local cuisine, sailing again the next morning.

Thirty-eight friends and family coming together to celebrate renewed all of our relationships. It was the trip of a lifetime!

When we returned to L.A., I said to Shawn, "It's interesting, but when we were on the boat, I thought I would have re-experienced that vision I had during my Ayahuasca journey—the one where I was sitting on a boat in a bikini, looking out at the sea and feeling so grateful. But that didn't happen."

I then forgot all about it until the following November, when we went on another trip, this time to the Grand Cayman Islands. My hair was growing back, though it was still very short. One afternoon, Shawn and I took an excursion on a small boat to swim with native fish in that area. I didn't want to go into the water, as most of the other people on the tour did. I was sitting by myself at the front edge of the boat with my feet dangling over the side, looking out at the gorgeous and glistening Caribbean Sea.

"God, everything is so beautiful," I said smiling to myself. "My life is beautiful. This day is beautiful. And I'm *cancer-free*. I did it!"

Feeling the sun on my skin, I looked down at my colorful new bikini, when my heart skipped a beat. *This* was the scene from the ceremony eleven months earlier that I had wondered about. It was the exact same scene with the exact same colorful bathing suit! My hair was growing back but still very short, *just as it was in the vision*. A surging wave of gratitude and tears of joy spilled down my cheeks. I sat there surrounded in comforting, glistening light, my heart filled with love. Once again, my Highest Self, through the transformational Ayahuasca medicine, had shown me my most probable future. I felt a shiver go down my spine. Just then, Shawn came out of the water and noticed me crying.

"What's wrong, Angel?" he asked in a concerned tone.

"Nothing is wrong at all. It's just that I realized a minute ago that—right here, right now—was the precise scene I saw in my journey! This is the bikini I was wearing in that vision, and I was looking out at the ocean, feeling the deepest sense of gratitude—just as I had seen! It's all good, my love."

CHAPTER 8

The Greatest Gift

Life changes dramatically and permanently after a cancer diagnosis. For me, cancer was the ultimate blessing in disguise—a blessing I needed to acknowledge. I learned how much I needed to heal from all the resentments that had been simmering under the surface. And the healing that began in my heart started to radiate outward, enhancing all of my relationships.

In three Aya ceremonies, I was inspired to write a book, something I certainly did not want to do. It had never occurred to me that my story would be worth putting on paper. During the last ceremony the message came in for the third time, and it was delivered loud and clear: "Write the book already!"

I finally decided to listen, and I am deeply touched that you as the reader might benefit from this truthful knowledge I gained through my extraordinary experiences.

Many people who battle cancer face a prolonged and exhausting journey to conquer this terrifying disease, and many individuals survive cancer—physically. And even though they have gone through chemo, radiation, surgery, or all three, somehow the cancer returns. I now believe that this is caused by not addressing and releasing the emotional wounds that contributed to creating this disease to begin with.

In this final chapter, I would like to share with you the most important lessons and insights that cancer brought into my life, and I sincerely hope that you will be inspired to begin your own inner exploration. Why wait until you have a life-threatening illness to uncover a fuller, more profound, and happier life?

Forgiveness Is The First Step Toward Emotional Healing

I learned that forgiveness was the first and most important step towards my recovery. According to research by Dr. Michael S. Barry, author of *The Forgiveness Project*, of all cancer patients studied, 61 percent have severe forgiveness issues. Similarly, throughout my Ayahuasca trips, I saw that I was carrying deeply buried resentments that were directly related to my having developed breast cancer.

In my experience, it can be very difficult to move into forgiveness after being hurt, manipulated, or even abused—especially if what happened is deemed unforgivable. Our moral and spiritual framework wants justice. Why should the person who harmed me be forgiven? They don't deserve it! They violated my trust. They should be punished for what they have done to me. I certainly did not want to let them off the hook with my forgiveness, while I continued to unfairly suffer the consequences of their actions.

Holding on to resentments and blame has certain "benefits." While in a relationship with Derick, my righteousness and anger were energizing, like an adrenaline rush, and gave me a feeling of superiority. It was very satisfying having my friends agree that my animosity was justified, in particular when Derick got our receptionist pregnant. Sometimes I even enjoyed fantasies of revenge and thought of "appropriate" ways to punish him, or I imagined other people punishing him for me.

Karen Swartz, M.D., a psychiatrist and director of the Mood Disorders Adult Consultation Clinic at the Johns Hopkins Hospital, wrote an excellent article called: "Forgiveness: Your Health Depends on It." She explains that the act of forgiveness can reap huge rewards for your health, lowering the risk of heart attack, reducing pain, blood pressure, levels of anxiety, depression, and stress. Forgiveness calms stress levels, leading to improved health.*

---

* Dr. Karen Swartz, "Forgiveness: Your Health Depends on It," Johns Hopkins Medicine, https://www.hopkinsmedicine.org/health/wellness-and-prevention/forgiveness-your-health-depends-on-it

Forgiveness is not something you do for the other person; forgiveness is something you do for yourself. You have to give up revenge for your own freedom.

According to research, anger and resentment raise adrenaline and cortisol hormones, putting ourselves into fight-or-flight mode. These hormones suppress the immune system and allow illness to easily invade our bodies. I believe that is what happened to me. The energy of resentment poisoned me. There is a saying that goes, "Resentment is like taking poison and waiting for the other person to die."

What I was shown while under the influence of the transformational plant medicine was that forgiveness simply meant that I was to refuse to devote any time and energy to the one who had harmed me. Resenting someone is an ongoing practice that can be very draining, and the act of forgiveness only requires that it be done once.

In no way did I dismiss that I had been hurt. But I saw that, without forgiveness, I could not release my negativity and therefore could not heal.

I was shocked when I realized just how much forgotten blame and animosity were still buried within me. I have always hated the victim mentality, so it was a rude awakening to discover that I was actively cultivating it myself!

It became clear to me that forgiving someone did not mean that I was excusing their actions or pardoning them.

It also did not mean that I had to openly tell the person that I had to forgive them. I realized that I might be perceived as self-righteous if I announced that I was graciously granting my "abuser" forgiveness, wanting to make him feel guilty, thus making myself feel superior.

So, How Do You Forgive Completely?

In one of my journeys, with my awareness expanded, five practical steps occurred to me that I needed to implement in order to forgive completely. Here are my five steps that do not involve drinking Ayahuasca:

Step One: Forgiveness begins with the *willingness to let go,* which takes immense courage. (The risk of forgiveness for me meant I might open myself up to being hurt again.)

Step Two: I needed to *be present* to the pain and to the impact the incident created. My emotions were legitimate, and I needed to *feel* them before they could be relinquished. I had to embrace them until I fully comprehended the effect they had upon me.

- I had to recognize and own these feelings.
- How did they damage me? How did they change me?
- What was I holding in my body? Grief, anger, sadness, hate, jealousy?
- I had to go back to the place and time when I closed down to protect my heart and be with all of that hurt.
- I had to have *compassion and love for myself* in that pain.

Be there for yourself and embrace yourself. Try to heal and retrieve the part of yourself that you left behind at the moment the pain originally happened. Give yourself permission to cry. You can vent your anger safely in your own home or with a therapist. Do whatever works for you. Remember, you can write a letter to the person involved. Do not send it, but destroy it afterwards. You can implement a powerful release ritual in the burning of it, as we did at the Optimum Health Institute.

Step Three: After I'd sat with the impact for a while, after I had owned the pain and acknowledged all of the feelings I experienced, I had to *try to somehow walk a little bit in the "abuser's" shoes.*

- What had to have occurred in their life that would have made them capable of doing something like *that* to me?

- What "messed up thing" did someone do to them that would have them treat me in such a cruel manner?

- I also had to ask myself, "What is this incident teaching me? What can I learn from this?" Possibly compassion, or true forgiveness? Maybe they are here to teach me *how important forgiveness really is.*

Step Four: I had to give myself permission to see the person who hurt me, in an entirely new light. *With compassion,* I reached out in thought and thanked them for the opportunity to heal myself. Finally, *I had empathy.* I now viewed them as someone healed of their own pain and freed from their own suffering.

This may seem impossible. You might still be thinking, *The person who hurt me, definitely doesn't deserve sympathy, but punishment.* They *hurt* me. *Why do I now have to have compassion for them?*

Remember, you are doing this for you—not them. If you continue to carry this burden, it will ultimately make you sick. Forgiving will become easier as you learn to flex those unused muscles, and soon you will be completely free.

When you *replace resentment with compassion,* you will find that there really is nothing to forgive.

Step Five: Know that *there is nothing to forgive,* and move on!

How do you know you have forgiven and that you have let go entirely? The answer is that you will stop rehearsing it. You will not be triggered by it; you will hardly even think of it. It will feel like a forgotten dream. You *want* true forgiveness. When I realized that there was nothing to forgive and that I only had compassion left, my heart opened, and I had more peace. Now I feel liberated and empowered.

Make a list of every person you need to forgive and do these five steps with each one of them.

Almost every Ayahuasca journey allowed me to go back in time to see and understand the pain and anger I still carried toward former boyfriends and even toward my parents and grandparents. Ayahuasca took me to the infinite place within me where I was able to see not only how I had been hurt and the impact it had on me, but it also taught me how to view things from the other person's perspective. I was able to recognize the roots of their behavior. I was able to feel true compassion for each person's own trials and conflicted childhoods.

In the mysterious realm of plant medicine, I could review and reprogram the painful events of my past in real time and begin to heal. For example, when I had the visions of being a sad and lonely little girl in Germany, I visualized my adult self, giving abundant love to my five-year-old self. In one vision, I actually saw several little Jasnas lying next to me and all around me. I could see myself simultaneously as an infant, at age one, age three, age five, age seven, and age eight. All of those "little girls" were with me, and I felt myself embracing and loving every one of them. I was able to nourish all my wounded childhood traumas by simply visualizing abundant joy for each and every precious little version of myself. Ever since my first Ayahuasca journey, my inner child has started to dance, and she hasn't stopped dancing and laughing since. That doesn't mean that I am always smiling, but she certainly is, and she is now a contributing part of who I am.

You can do the same for yourself without Ayahuasca. Perhaps you can visualize and love your inner child during meditation or right before you go to sleep. Setting an intention just before sleep can be very effective. During that time, your mind is in an extremely powerful theta brainwave state.

Revisiting those difficult times in order to release the pain will expand your heart. Eventually, you will regain harmony and balance, just as I did.

Self-Forgiveness Is the Most Difficult Form of Forgiveness

For me, the most difficult form of forgiveness was self-forgiveness. Once I had sincerely and thoroughly forgiven all the people on my list, I needed to grant myself forgiveness. This was much more arduous because guilt was the hardest thing to let go off.

The day I was diagnosed, I suddenly understood that, when my mother had breast cancer several years earlier, I had been too wrapped up in my own tedious dramas and jealousies to offer her the loving attention and support she deserved. Although she had come to the United States for several months of treatment and we'd all helped to take care of her physically, looking back, I saw that I had not been there for her emotionally.

How could I have failed my mother in this way? I loved her so much! Where were my priorities? I cried and cried over it. Now knowing what it meant to be diagnosed with cancer, I felt so guilty and just couldn't forgive myself for letting her down like that. What a torturous nightmare it must have been for her. She must have felt so alone and isolated. From a shattered, broken place, I called her and apologized profusely.

"You did the best you could, Sweetheart, and you were going through such a rough time. There is nothing to forgive. I never once thought about it. Don't be hard on yourself. You need to focus on your own health now. I love you so much," my mother affectionately said.

I finally decided to listen to her and to be generous with myself. I reached for self-compassion to have empathy and forgiveness for myself. I had to acknowledge my wrongdoing and own up to my mistakes, and then let them go.

You, too, can humbly accept what has transpired despite what you think you may have done or not done. You don't need to rationalize or justify it. Everyone makes bad choices. There is so much guilt and shame that we all carry, and we need to access generosity and compassion towards ourselves in order to forgive. We cannot have self-love without self-compassion. Many of us judge ourselves harshly and unfairly. I know I did!

Self-forgiveness didn't mean that I was simply accepting my past behavior and letting myself off the hook either. I was taking authentic responsibility for my actions, opting to leave the past behind and move on. Yes, I have screwed up, but making it a learning experience has allowed me to excel in unexpected ways. I faced my feelings of remorse and guilt, and then made amends for my behavior.

If you are ready to forgive yourself, you can process your own feelings one last time by writing yourself a letter, followed by a burning ritual, symbolically letting it all go. Then you need to *have self-compassion*. Without the burden of self-hatred, you too can transform your life and experience enormous freedom.

Ayahuasca is only one modality for personal transformation. There are many other ways to facilitate forgiveness and emotional healing. You don't need to drink one of the most powerful plant medicines to get there. Other plants like cannabis, used in ceremonial settings with clear intentions, can be surprisingly healing and provide deep insights. Many get answers through meditation. Hundreds of published research studies document that Transcendental Meditation delivers a wide range of benefits. You can also find a variety of forgiveness rituals and ceremonies online.

My time spent facing the possibility of death for two years taught me that underneath all my self-protectiveness and defensiveness lay the yearning to connect and to love. My life, like yours, is dictated by the choices we make moment by moment. Join me in making a choice to forgive, and it will lead us all to an empowering path that will bring more harmony to our planet.

Self-Love Is Not Selfish

Being confronted with Stage 3 cancer allowed me to discover that *the love of one's self is the most important and highest form of love there is*. Loving myself isn't merely liking myself. It can seem selfish, but I learned that I can only love another to the extent that I can love myself. It essentially means that I am determined to no longer sacrifice my well-being to please others. Instead, I now have high regard, acceptance, and appreciation for my own happiness. During a TED talk, Anita Moorjani, the author of *Dying To Be Me* said, "Love yourself like your life depends on it, because it does."

Can you have too much love for another? Of course not. In the same way, you can never have too much love for yourself. Loving myself allows me to love others more fully and deeply. I practice self-love each day and focus on honoring my true self. If there is something I would have previously criticized, I now accept it. For instance, I really don't like my thin hair, and I was hoping it would come back full and curly after chemo, but it didn't. Every morning after I dry my hair, I think gratefully, "At least I have hair!"

I no longer compare myself to others, and I treat my body with great care and respect.

There are many ways to practice self-love. I ask myself every day: *What can I do to make myself happier and more joyful today? What can I do to show the love I have for myself?* I don't feel guilty when I do things that make me happy. I not only listen to my feelings, but I also value them and speak them aloud—something I have never done before. I am not concerned about appearing weak or less than perfect. I take responsibility, and I choose to surround myself with good friends and environments that empower me.

I also practice writing and *feeling* positive "I am" statements, and continue to say kind things to myself whenever I look in the mirror. I have fired the "little devil" on my shoulder that used to constantly chastise me. *Love is a verb; it's something we do.* My stronger sense of self-love allows me to love my husband with greater intensity, and our love is now based on an even stronger foundation.

Cancer Helped Me Reassess My Priorities

Those of us who are cancer survivors know all too well that cancer and the thought of death go hand in hand. Before my diagnosis, I would have told anyone that I was happier than I had ever been before. Yet cancer underscored the depth of my passion for life and gave me a new awareness of how acutely, even desperately, I wanted to live. Wouldn't it be ideal if we were all wholly dedicated to being completely present in every precious moment?

My priorities have shifted from an emphasis on *doing* to an emphasis on *being*. I have become more patient and less competitive. I have learned how to be more vulnerable and more open. Living with a vulnerable heart, I feel more connected to people around me and now have a desire to be of service.

My brother, Vladimir, was one of the first to notice the change in me. Close to the end of my chemotherapy treatments, he said, "You have always been a powerful, confident woman who could accomplish anything you wanted. No task was too big, too expensive, or too intimidating for you. But since your illness, you are focused more on family and connecting with the people you love. I think this has helped you discover an even greater, more magical quality in your feminine power."

I was very touched by Vladimir's affirmation. The threat of cancer made it crystal clear that every moment of my life is sacred and purposeful. I have become more present with my clients, allowing more time to listen to them than I used to. They feel heard, and because of this, they are happier with the results of my treatments, and I now have more client referrals than ever.

I used to rush through life, always pursuing the next activity, experience, or purchase. Now I take joy in the small things—having coffee with my husband on our patio, listening to a friend tell me about her date, walking along the beach at a leisurely pace, or savoring the beauty around me.

Gratitude Is My Medicine

One of my ultimate gifts from cancer is this deeper appreciation for life in general. I am reminded to count my blessings every day and to embrace the act of gratitude. This is still my key to a rewarding and even happier life.

Countless people live in a world of cancer phobia. Fear of recurrence is common amongst cancer survivors, and it can be scary and difficult to live with the fact that it could come back. Sometimes negative thoughts get the best of me too. I am still confronted with those dark places, but I have the awareness of it all now. Even though those thoughts rarely show up, I always acknowledge them and try not to let them linger. I don't consider allowing myself to feel my fears to be the opposite of having a positive attitude. It simply validates that I have them. I try to be aware of what triggers my worry of recurrence. It could be a commercial on TV about a cancer drug or hearing that someone passed away from cancer. I try not to let that control me and affect my quality of life. I change my focus away from it—after a brief review—and then move on.

As you read in the prior pages, I made changes and adjustments in my life to manage my cancer diagnosis. When I was going through treatments, it was hard to maintain a state of optimism regarding my "divine health opportunity." This made it all the more crucial for me to instill gratitude as a daily practice. I kept a journal on everything I felt was important for me to embrace—my wonderful marriage, a strong support network, freshly brewed coffee each morning, and the smile on my husband's face when he first awakens.

The physical action of writing and speaking statements of gratitude helped me internalize these feelings. Now that I am free of my old wounds, I experience life with more excitement and clarity. I can't predict the future, but I can try to enjoy each moment with joy.

Even though cancer is "past tense" in our lives, Shawn and I both keep our gratitude practice on track. We always start our morning routine by expressing our appreciation for each other. When Shawn wakes up—usually before I do—he whispers, "Another day to be together, Angel!"

We make a point to remain connected to each other, no matter how busy we seem to be, and always confirm our love for each other. We also set intentions for the great day we are about to have. There is power in the spoken word, and repetition of positive ideas is sure to create a positive mind-set. Because Shawn works from home, we have the luxury of seeing each other throughout the day. We pause to kiss several times a day, and before we go to sleep, we share three or four things for which we are grateful for that day.

Gratitude is a strong path to lifting my spirit and shifting my energy by simply making a conscious effort to pay attention to something I am thankful for. At one of his seminars, Tony Robbins said, "If you can *feel* gratitude for something for only three minutes, it will shift your energy into happiness." During illness, for example, you can express gratitude for a doctor you trust, for your optimistic attitude, for supportive family and friends, or for moments with no pain or fatigue.

If you are not ill, can you still find something to be grateful for? Maybe you face other challenges, such as loneliness, a tedious job, chronic migraines, or some other ongoing issue. How can you identify things to appreciate? I just pause, take a deep breath, look around, and find one thing, big or small (and really, those small things often *are* the big things), I could be thankful for. *It's another beautiful, sunny day, and I live in California!* That thought usually makes me feel particularly fortunate.

Maybe you have a dog that you can pet, making you feel better right away. Perhaps you woke up and had a good night's sleep in your comfortable bed. You have to start somewhere and once you get going, you will be amazed by how your list grows. Nothing that I enjoy in life, even finding a parking spot in a crowded lot, is too insignificant for me to feel gratitude for. I highly recommend that you write down three to five things you genuinely feel thankful for every single day.

Even now that I am complete with cancer, I continue to say to myself, "I am so grateful for the health of my body. Thank you!"

The Mind-Body Connection Is Indivisible

The mind-body connection is well established, and I do not believe that it is possible to separate physical health from emotional health. I am pleased by and proud of approaching my cancer from all sides—emotionally, spiritually, mentally, and physically, with both alternative and conventional medicine.

I know some people might wonder, "What good were all those cleanses, raw foods, sprouts, and mind-altering plants when you had surgery and did chemotherapy anyway?" That is a very legitimate question.

My answer is this: The healing within my heart, the learning of forgiveness and the act of self-love, opened the gateway for all my cancer treatments—both alternative and Western medicine—to work. Ayahuasca prompted me to explore hidden pains and to release them for good, and this emotional freedom made the space necessary for my physical healing.

And while I am deeply grateful for the chemotherapy that killed all of the cancer cells in my body and helped me heal physically, it was Ayahuasca that made complete healing possible. She activated areas in my brain that were hidden, allowing me to witness things that were clearly unknown to me, in order to release long-forgotten memories and pains. This led to the indispensable healing of significant traumas and resentments.

All the things I explored were milestones on a life-changing path of self-discovery. **The body cannot regain its health if the soul is suffering.**

Receiving Is Another Way of Giving

Before my illness, my identity was wrapped up in being a doer, an achiever, and a giver. I was always uncomfortable in the role of receiver, even of compliments. What I discovered was that the typical cancer mentality for women is, "I don't want to be a burden." It is much easier for us to give love than to receive love.

But, as a cancer patient, I was in a weakened condition. I had to sit still and learn to receive, especially during chemo. Paige selflessly helped organize the Food Angels program that brought meals to us for several months during the worst of it. This allowed me to become better at receiving, when so many wonderful people wanted to help. They demonstrated abundant care, and eventually I understood that in the act of receiving what others wanted to give, I was both the receiver *and* the giver. Finally, I learned what Shawn had been trying to teach me—that in the act of receiving what others wanted to give, I became a giver by sincerely acknowledging their contribution. Of course, there is also the added benefit that when you give to others, you are also giving to yourself.

As children in Croatia, we never received compliments. It's funny that the word *acknowledgment* does not even exist in the Croatian language. This may be one reason I made a habit of deflecting acknowledgment of my achievements, or compliments about my appearance, or anything else someone would appreciate about me. I was always uneasy when the focus was directed at me.

Cancer taught me that I needed to be more present and to pay attention to what others were really trying to tell me. I learned that in rejecting or denying a sincere compliment,

I was actually being dismissive of that person: "You think I look pretty? I can't imagine why. It's a bad hair day for me!" I realized that accepting admiration is a way of honoring the other person as they kindly offer the gift of acknowledgment. Now I receive a compliment, or anything else someone wants to gift me, with a warm and sincere "Thank you."

I also had to allow myself to become more vulnerable, something else that had always been a challenge. I grew up with a strong sense of self-reliance. From young adulthood, I was a capable and dependable person whom others could rely on. Yet, I had a need to control my environment and even to control others, which made me somewhat masculine. Naturally, I wanted to be desired as a woman by the men in my life, but my insistence on being in the giver role, rather than the softer, *receiver* role, had cost me some vital aspect of my femininity. It shut down my receptivity to the concept of vulnerability.

Derick and I had built a company from nothing, eventually growing it to more than sixty employees. I was the CEO not only at work, but also at home. Our masculine and feminine polarities were out of adjustment, and as a result, there was no space for real intimacy. Of course, that relationship was never healthy from the start.

When I first met Shawn, we had both already discovered the masculine and feminine polarities taught by David Deida,

Justin Sterling, and Dr. Pat Allen. Shawn's instinctual masculine traits allowed me to finally let my guard down. This helped me to reclaim my feminine essence and to receive his masculine gifts with more ease.

Nowadays, it seems that women tend to be more masculine than feminine in their relationships. And, as women, we are often compelled (understandably) to call upon our masculine side in order to achieve success in our work environment. As Dr. Pat Allen and David Deida explain, our masculine traits diminish intimacy with our partner. The masculine and feminine energies are like magnets drawn towards each other. Therefore, the greater the polarity, the greater the attraction, chemistry, and passion will be. Without polarity there is no intimacy.

Shawn and I are both very aware of that, and we honor and cultivate these energies. From our first date, he made me feel like a lady, when he securely took my hand to cross the street and opened the car door for me. I enjoy letting him take the lead, which allows me to embrace my softer feminine side so that I can be more relaxed and playful. He drives however he wants, takes any wrong exit he chooses to, and pushes the elevator button every time we're together. Those small things make him feel like a king, and we both get to practice keeping the masculine and feminine balance between us. "He wears the pants, and I wear the panties."

Shawn helped me feel safe while being vulnerable. He takes care of my heart and honors my emotions, and in return

I trust, respect, and appreciate him greatly. *I learned that the real power of a woman lies within her heart.*

Surviving cancer is a huge accomplishment, and with it comes enormous inner strength. All my healing at the core allowed me to become the best version of myself. I would have never, in a million years, have guessed that cancer would teach me so much or that it could have expanded my heart, enlightened my mind, changed my outlook, and improved my world immensely.

Cancer was trying to tell me something, and I chose to listen. The natural intelligence within us that gives us life is the greatest healer on earth. *Cancer didn't happen TO me; Cancer happened FOR me.*

Sometimes I have to stop and marvel, "I am healthy! I don't have cancer!" Feeling gratitude, no matter what seems to be occurring is a choice, and making that choice opens my heart instantly and changes everything.

* * *

Carl G. Jung summed up my cancer journey beautifully, "Your vision will become clear only when you look inside your heart. Who looks outside, dreams. Who looks inside, awakens."

Cancer was truly a divine tap on my shoulder.

Thank you, Cancer.

Acknowledgments

This is my favorite part. I get to acknowledge and express my deep appreciation for everyone involved in helping me create this book.

But first—My humble, utmost respect, and deepest of gratitude to the most transformational plant medicine on Earth, Mother Ayahuasca.

To my husband Shawn—I feel so fortunate and blessed to have you by my side and to love you the way that I do. From the beginning, you have opened and nurtured my heart in ways I could only dream of. You have wiped my tears many times, and you have kept me strong during our intense two-year journey. I know that without your love and support, I wouldn't have healed in the way that I did. I continue to fall in love with you, my Warrior King.

To my amazing family—We might be scattered all around the world, but that doesn't take away from our closeness. I can count on your being there for me anytime, any day, even if it means drinking Ayahuasca together!

To my beautiful sister Zana—You supported me tremendously, not just in my cancer journey, but with this book as well. Your input was invaluable, and I love you so much.

To my gregarious brother Vladimir—You know how to make us all laugh no matter how difficult the times may be, making our troubles always feel a little lighter.

To my wonderful and brave mother—You are the one who knows what it means to be diagnosed with cancer. I love you enormously! Your commitment to spiritual growth and emotional healing is unwavering and such an inspiration to us all! You gave me the greatest gift, and words cannot describe how grateful I am to have experienced our profound Ayahuasca journeys together.

To my remarkable father—I felt your unconditional love, compassion, and immense worry throughout my illness, no matter how far apart we were. You were with me in spirit all that time. I love you so much!

To Paige and Maddy—The two best step-daughters any woman can hope for! I am blessed to have you both.

Paige—Your deep love, immense compassion, and hard work throughout my chemo treatments touched me beyond words. I can't thank you enough for who you are and for everything you did for me. The Food Angels project you created taught me to receive unconditionally, and I am deeply grateful for you and for the close relationship we have.

Maddy—Even though you were away at college most of the time, I could feel your love, and fear, not just for me, but for your dad too. You have such a beautiful heart, and I can't wait to see the amazing things you will create in your future. I am so proud of you and so happy to be part of it all.

To Ashley—Although you are my sister's daughter, I feel as if you are mine. I love you so much, and I am so proud of the powerful woman you have become. Your commitment to personal growth and your bravery to dive into the mysterious world of plant medicine is remarkable. You kept inspiring me to write this book over and over again. Thank you for that!

To Lluis—I am without words . . . You are the first person who told me, "Deep within you is the answer." Your commitment to my emotional healing and your huge generosity led me on this life-changing path. I can't express enough how deeply grateful I am to you, dearest Lluis!

To Briana—I knew from the moment I met you that you are the most powerful and bravest person I will ever know. Conquering your darkest demons was the utmost inspiration for me. Your commitment to healing and empowering women is deeply moving. You brought the greatest plant medicine to our entire family and provided the space for enormous healing—not just my cancer healing but emotional family healing as well. Words cannot describe the depth of gratitude I feel for you, my beautiful Spirit Sister.

To Leara—I am so grateful for your unwavering support regarding my health. You were not just there for me emotionally and mentally for two long years, but you supported me physically with your amazing product line that you so generously provided. I know how important it is to take the purest vitamins, and I feel very confident that your Frequency Foods supplements helped me immensely throughout. They made a big difference in my rapid healing after surgery. I love you, and I love your products!

To the same Leara, who was my Chief Editor for this book—Thank you so much for helping me bring my words more to life. You always knew exactly what I was trying to say. You are a great friend, Leara, and I don't know what I would have done without you. I am so happy that you and Dan are part of our life.

To Wayne and Margot—Our dearest friends who we were destined to meet!

Wayne—I love your enthusiasm for your spiritual work, and I am deeply grateful for your dedication and for what you and Margot have contributed to me and my family.

Margot—I will never forget your sympathetic and emotional support right before my surgery. You were lying next to me, holding me, and crying with me in my harshest despair. I genuinely admire your selfless service and I am so happy to be your friend.

To John and my beautiful bestie, Christy—Even though we met when I was almost done with my cancer journey, your friendship has changed my day-to-day happiness. Cancer brought us together, and that is another great gift I get to enjoy. Your spiritual work and your friendship mean the world to us. I love you, Christyne.

To Russell—Thank you for bringing Briana into our life. You insisted on being of service, and you provided the space for me, my mom, and my sister to overcome pains we didn't even knew where there.

To my Aunt Goga in Croatia—Thank you for your love, support, and worry. You have been there for me every time I have needed your advice. I love you!

To Judy—I am so grateful for your generous input and contribution to my book.

To Dr. Takasugi—I am deeply grateful for your enormous patience with me and for not giving up on me. I thank you for your unwavering commitment to women's health and their lives. You have been the kindest and most compassionate doctor throughout my journey. I wish you all the best that life has to offer.

To Dr. Ferreira—Thank you for being a great oncologist and keeping me on track. You prescribed the perfect "cocktail" for me!

To Dr. Klausmeyer—Thank you for giving me the perfect look. You are a wonderful and very kind plastic surgeon.

To Ty and Charlene Bollinger— Thank you for creating The Truth About Cancer documentary! Your enormous and brave commitment to providing crucial information about alternative cancer healing gave me hope and inspired my journey to look outside the box of conventional treatments. I am deeply grateful for your selfless work!

To Dr. Lodi—Thank you for your commitment to alternative cancer healing and for building An Oasis of Healing in Arizona. Your insightful phrase, "Cancer is a divine tap on your shoulder" has remained with me like a mantra ever since you told it to me.

To Landmark Education—Thank you for shifting and transforming the world one person at a time!

To David Deida, Dr. Pat Allen, and Justin Sterling—Thank you for teaching my husband to stand in his masculine power, and for bringing out the beautiful feminine goddess within me.

Resources

- **AtlasPROfilax.org**

  I absolutely love my job! I cannot thank my father enough for insisting that I get trained in this amazing healing method. AtlasPROfilax is a safe, non-invasive method that offers immediate and lasting results in usually only one session. This is achieved using a specially designed device that resets the muscle around the first cervical vertebra, eliminating headaches, migraines, vertigo, and neck stiffness, amongst other ailments.

- **blessedcancer.com & jasnaclancy.com**

  My personal websites for more information about my journey.

- **FrequencyFoods.com**

  I learned how important it was to take the correct vitamin C, as most vitamin C on the market is not of high quality. Their vitamin C is incredible! Same with their probiotics.

I continue to take their supplements, and know they make a huge difference and are essential for optimal health.

- ***QHHT®—Quantum Healing Hypnosis Technique by Dolores Cannon***

- **BQH—Beyond Quantum Healing by Candace Craw-Goldman**
  These are other great ways to explore deeper levels of consciousness and get profound insights into healing. They are loosely based on what most people may know as "past life regression." They are beautiful, gentle ways to connect with higher aspects of yourself without using plant medicine. You can find many videos on QHHT and BQH sessions on YouTube.

- **Optimum Health Institute**
  This is a great holistic healing place with a powerful and intense three week program for mind, body and spirit! I felt thoroughly cleansed, physically and emotionally. Afterwards, I was inspired and motivated to make more appropriate health choices.

- **An Oasis of Healing—Dr. Lodi**
  This is a great, inspiring healing facility that integrates alternative and conventional medicine for cancer treatments.

- **Rythmia—Costa Rica**

  Rythmia is the only five-star, all-inclusive, medically licensed luxury resort and retreat center in the world that offers Ayahuasca ceremonies. They are located in beautiful Guanacaste, Costa Rica.

- **More Great Resources**

  - *Dying to be Me* — Anita Moorjani
  - *When the Body Says No* — Dr. Gabor Maté
  - *How to Change Your Mind* — Michael Polland
  - *Forgiveness: Your Health Depends on It* — Article by Dr. Karen Swartz
  - *The Law of Attraction* — Ester and Jerry Hicks
  - *You Can Heal Your Life* — Louise Hay
  - *Strength in Stillness*: *The Power of Transcendental Meditation* — Bob Roth
  - *Conversations with God: An Uncommon Dialogue* — Neale Donald Walsch
  - *The Truth About Cancer* — Documentary by Ty and Charlene Bollinger